The Plight
of the Thrift Institutions

Studies in the Regulation of Economic Activity
TITLES PUBLISHED

Studies in the Regulation of Economic Activity

The Plight
of the Thrift Institutions

Andrew S. Carron

THE BROOKINGS INSTITUTION
Washington, D.C.

Library of Congress Cataloging in Publication data:
Carron, Andrew S.
  The plight of the thrift institutions.
  (Studies in the regulation of economic activity)
  Includes bibliographical references and index.
  1. Building and loan associations—United
States.   2. Savings banks—United States.
3. Credit unions—United States.   4. Financial
institutions—United States—State supervision.
I. Title.   II. Series.
HG2152.C37   332.2'0973   81-71434
ISBN 0-8157-1300-2   AACR2
ISBN 0-8157-1299-5 (pbk.)

1 2 3 4 5 6 7 8 9

THE BROOKINGS INSTITUTION is an independent organization devoted to nonpartisan research, education, and publication in economics, government, foreign policy, and the social sciences generally. Its principal purposes are to aid in the development of sound public policies and to promote public understanding of issues of national importance.

The Institution was founded on December 8, 1927, to merge the activities of the Institute for Government Research, founded in 1916, the Institute of Economics, founded in 1922, and the Robert Brookings Graduate School of Economics and Government, founded in 1924.

The Board of Trustees is responsible for the general administration of the Institution, while the immediate direction of the policies, program, and staff is vested in the President, assisted by an advisory committee of the officers and staff. The by-laws of the Institution state: "It is the function of the Trustees to make possible the conduct of scientific research, and publication, under the most favorable conditions, and to safeguard the independence of the research staff in the pursuit of their studies and in the publication of the results of such studies. It is not a part of their function to determine, control, or influence the conduct of particular investigations or the conclusions reached."

The President bears final responsibility for the decision to publish a manuscript as a Brookings book. In reaching his judgment on the competence, accuracy, and objectivity of each study, the President is advised by the director of the appropriate research program and weighs the views of a panel of expert outside readers who report to him in confidence on the quality of the work. Publication of a work signifies that it is deemed a competent treatment worthy of public consideration but does not imply endorsement of conclusions or recommendations.

The Institution maintains its position of neutrality on issues of public policy in order to safeguard the intellectual freedom of the staff. Hence interpretations or conclusions in Brookings publications should be understood to be solely those of the authors and should not be attributed to the Institution, to its trustees, officers, or other staff members, or to the organizations that support its research.

Foreword

Since the Depression, savings and loan associations and mutual savings banks have been the principal repositories of household financial savings and the major sources of residential mortgage credit. Operating for most of that time in a protective web of regulations and a climate of stable interest rates, these thrift institutions performed the function of intermediation— accepting small short-term deposits to make large long-term loans. The system began to change in 1966, however, when ceilings on deposit interest rates were first applied to thrift institutions. The industry flourished for at least ten years after that, but a serious crisis was building. When market interest rates rose sharply in the late 1970s, the legacy of governmental regulation pushed many firms near insolvency, and the entire thrift industry was seriously weakened.

The problem for the thrift institutions and the government agencies that insure their deposits is to manage the transition to deregulation while preserving deposit-taking and mortgage-lending services for the household sector. The challenge is to do so while maintaining public confidence in the nation's financial system, making efficient use of government resources, and avoiding the imposition of new regulations that could ultimately hinder rather than aid the adjustment process.

In this book Andrew S. Carron reviews the recent performance of the thrift industry and assesses its outlook under various sets of economic assumptions. He estimates the amount of financial assistance the industry will require and describes the forces compelling its structural consolidation. A chapter is devoted to an analysis of options available to the government, including tax and regulatory alternatives. The book concludes with recommendations for policy.

Andrew Carron is a research associate in the Brookings Economic Studies program. He is grateful to Suzanne M. Wehrs for providing research assistance, to John Karl Scholz for calculating the effects of various tax policies, and to the Social Science Computation Center for data-processing assistance. Barry P. Bosworth, Anthony Downs, Robert Kalish,

Michael Moran and others offered helpful comments on the manuscript. This study could not have been completed without the cooperation of many individuals in the thrift industry and its trade associations, and the federal regulatory agencies. Nancy D. Davidson edited the manuscript; Penelope Harpold checked it for accuracy.

This is the eighteenth publication in the Brookings series of Studies in the Regulation of Economic Activity. The series presents the results of research on public policies toward business. The study was funded by grants from the Ford Foundation, the Alfred P. Sloan Foundation, and the Alex C. Walker Educational and Charitable Foundation.

The views expressed here are those of the author and should not be ascribed to the foundations whose assistance is acknowledged above or to the trustees, officers, or other staff members of the Brookings Institution.

BRUCE K. MAC LAURY
President

Washington, D.C.
November 1981

Contents

Tables

Figures

Chapter One

The Problems

Highly developed financial markets and institutions have been major contributors to U.S. economic growth and financial stability during the past three decades. In particular, savings and loan associations and mutual savings banks encouraged thrift and provided mortgage funds for home buyers. A web of regulatory structures was installed to help maintain the safety and soundness of these financial institutions and to promote certain income distribution goals. Since the mid-1960s, however, changes have occurred in the underlying economic situation and in the investment behavior of individuals and institutions. In 1980, the thrift industry began losing money for the first time since the Depression, and losses accelerated in 1981. The rate of home construction fell to a thirty-five-year low. Regulatory authorities reacted to developments in a piecemeal fashion at first, creating significant inefficiencies and distributional distortions. Only recently, in the context of a regulatory reform movement ranging across product and service industries, have there been attempts at comprehensive reform in the regulation of financial markets. Nevertheless, the short-term problems of the thrift institutions persist.

Operation and Insurance

Three types of financial intermediaries are referred to as thrift institutions: savings and loan associations, mutual savings banks, and credit unions. Thrift institutions have traditionally earned their profits and paid their operating expenses through denomination and maturity intermediation—purchasing small short-term deposits with low interest rates to make large long-term loans at higher interest rates. So, unlike direct capital market investments where the lender's asset is identical to the borrower's liability, there is a maturity imbalance for the financial intermediary. The risks are that deposits may be withdrawn unexpectedly, leading to illiquidity, and that there may be unforeseen increases in interest rates, raising the

1

possibility of insolvency. Moreover, the rate charged on loans may be artificially depressed by usury ceilings or by laws and regulations that prevent thrift institutions from investing their assets elsewhere (an excess supply of funds in the mortgage market would reduce the interest rate on mortgages).[1]

Institutions maintain a large net worth to provide reserves that can be drawn upon during periods of reduced liquidity or high interest rates, such as may occur over a business cycle. Should those reserves prove insufficient, however, the risk ultimately would be shifted to the depositor because these firms have mutual or limited-liability stock forms of organization. Savers ordinarily would be reluctant to make deposits under these circumstances, so commercial banks and thrift institutions carry deposit insurance. In the event of insolvency or a severe liquidity shortage, the insuror would take responsibility for depositors' accounts and assume control of the institution's assets.

Thrift institutions are regulated under laws of the states and the federal government. State institutions are chartered under state statutes and are supervised and examined by agencies of the state government. Institutions also have the option of a federal charter.

Savings and loan associations—which are also called building and loan associations, cooperative banks, homestead associations, building associations, and savings associations—accept deposits primarily from the household sector. Associations then use these funds to make loans, primarily for residential mortgages. The terms under which savings and loans are chartered, as well as provisions of the federal tax law, have limited the extent to which assets could be invested in other instruments; regulatory changes in 1980 and 1981 somewhat relaxed these restrictions. Most savings and loan associations (83 percent), representing 75 percent of savings and loan assets, have a mutual form of organization under which the depositors are the owners. The remainder are stockholder-owned.[2]

There are 4,613 savings and loan associations with total assets of $629.8 billion. Deposits at 4,002 of them (representing 98.2 percent of the assets) are insured by the Federal Savings and Loan Insurance Corporation

1. See Patric H. Hendershott and Kevin E. Villani, *Regulation and Reform of the Housing Finance System* (Washington, D.C.: American Enterprise Institute for Public Policy Research, 1977), pp. 15–16.

2. U.S. League of Savings Associations, *Savings and Loan Fact Book '80* (Chicago: USLSA, 1980), pp. 51–52.

(FSLIC), a federal agency established in 1934 as part of the Federal Home Loan Bank Board.[3] Its insurance fund has been built up from premiums paid by members and from investment earnings on those premiums. Roughly half of the FSLIC-insured institutions are "federal" savings and loan associations, chartered under provisions of the Home Owners' Loan Act of 1933 and supervised by the Federal Home Loan Bank Board.

The 611 savings and loan associations without FSLIC insurance are state-chartered firms located in four states—Maryland, Massachusetts, North Carolina, and Ohio—and insured by private corporations. Although comprising 13 percent of the institutions, the state-insured associations are relatively small, holding only 1.8 percent of savings and loan assets.

All mutual savings banks have a mutual form of charter. They are concentrated in the Middle Atlantic and New England regions, although they are also found in the West. Like the savings and loans, mutual savings banks invest primarily in residential mortgages, although they have somewhat more flexibility. There are 463 mutual savings banks with total assets of $171.6 billion.[4] Deposits at most mutual savings banks are insured by the Federal Deposit Insurance Corporation (FDIC), the same entity that insures deposits at most commercial banks. (Some savings banks in Massachusetts have their deposits insured by the Mutual Savings Central Fund, Inc., and the three federally chartered mutual savings banks are insured by the FSLIC.)[5] Like the FSLIC, the FDIC was established during the Depression and is supported by insurance premiums and investment earnings.

Credit unions are mutual institutions and are the smallest and most specialized of the financial intermediaries. They accept deposits and make loans only for members of a group with a common bond—generally the employees of a firm or members of a labor union. Credit union assets are invested primarily in short-term consumer loans and direct credit market instruments. There are 21,915 credit unions with $71.9 billion in assets.[6] Credit union deposits are insured by the National Credit Union Administration or by state-chartered insurance corporations.

3. Federal Home Loan Bank Board, "Savings and Loan Activity in July," August 28, 1981, table 5. Figures are for year-end 1980.

4. National Association of Mutual Savings Banks, *1981 National Fact Book of Mutual Savings Banking* (New York: NAMSB, 1981), table 2, p. 11. Figures are for year-end 1980.

5. See ibid., table 7, p. 14.

6. National Credit Union Administration, "Credit Union Statistics: Selected Data for January 1981," March 3, 1981. Figures are for year-end 1980.

Figure 1-1. *Deposit Rate Ceilings at Thrift Institutions and Market Interest Rates, 1966–80*

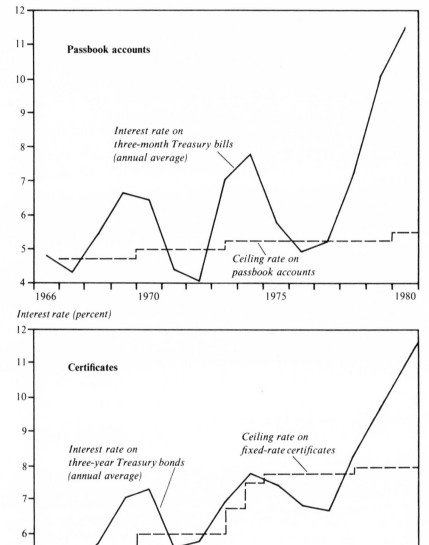

Sources: *Economic Report of the President, 1981*, pp. 308–09; and *Federal Reserve Bulletin* (various issues), table 1.16.

History of Regulation

Depository institutions—banks, savings and loan associations, mutual savings banks, and credit unions—have suffered a number of shocks in recent years, while their ability to adapt has been constrained by regulation. The problems began with inflation that was higher and more variable than in the past. Market interest rates moved up in concert, while various regulations restricted the extent to which nominal yields on both assets and liabilities could adjust to the inflation. In the past, government regulations helped to hold the cost of funds below the return on assets. The Federal Reserve Board's Regulation Q set the maximum rates that commercial banks were permitted to pay on time and savings deposits. These ceilings were raised along with market rates, and so were generally not binding constraints, until 1966. Rates at thrift institutions, not then subject to rate ceilings, were slightly higher than at commercial banks to offset the advantages of additional services available at banks. Thrifts were not permitted to offer checking accounts. Banks could offer these accounts, often called demand deposits or transaction accounts, but other regulations prohibited the payment of interest on them.

In 1966 there was a fundamental change of policy, flowing principally from a concern about the ability of the thrift institutions to pay the increasing rates on deposits and thereby maintain their role as the principal financial intermediaries for the housing industry. Since that time, deposit rate ceilings have been applied not only to commercial banks, but to savings and loan associations, mutual savings banks, and credit unions as well.[7] Despite periodic increases, these rate maxima have generally remained below market rates of interest (see figure 1-1). For that reason, and because the ceilings provide a focal point for competition, institutions have usually paid the highest interest rate permitted on any given class of deposit.

Two types of rate ceilings were imposed: a maximum allowable rate for each type of account affected depository institutions as a group vis-à-vis other instruments and institutions, and a differential was established so that the ceiling rates for thrifts were above those for banks. This was done to induce depositors to keep their savings accounts at thrifts even though their checking accounts were at commercial banks. Originally 0.75 to 1.00 percent, but later reduced to 0.50 percent in 1970 and to 0.25 in 1973, the

7. See Donald D. Hester, "Innovations and Monetary Control," *Brookings Papers on Economic Activity, 1:1981*, pp. 146–53.

Figure 1-2. *Account Structure at Savings and Loan Associations, 1966–81*

Billions of dollars

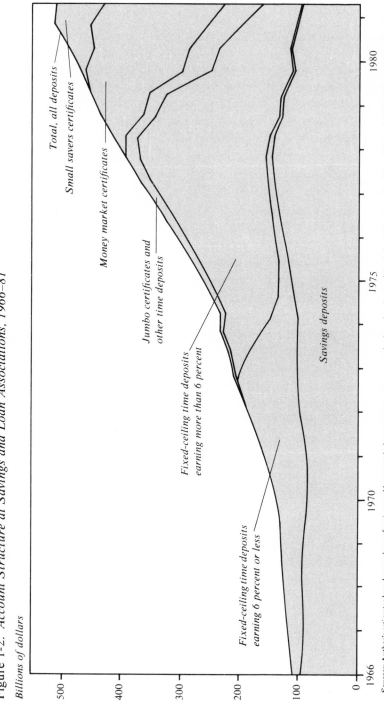

Sources: Author's estimates based on analyses of savings and loan association account structure appearing in various issues of the *Federal Home Loan Bank Board Journal*, 1973–81; Federal Home Loan Bank Board, *Savings and Home Financing Source Book*, 1978–80; and FHLBB, "Savings and Loan Activity in September," October 30, 1981.

differential was created to preserve the ability of thrifts to provide housing finance.

The effect of the deposit ceilings was twofold: as housing policy, the ceilings reduced the cost of the institutions' liabilities; and as monetary policy, ceilings provided a mechanism—through the effect of disintermediation on residential construction—for slowing economic expansion.[8] Because the government regulatory agencies could not control quantities, depositors withdrew their funds when interest rates rose and put them into instruments that may have been less convenient, but earned more interest. The cost of funds to thrift institutions was reduced, but so was the quantity. Thus rate ceilings served the goals of both housing policy and monetary policy, although the effect on the supply of savings was deleterious to housing.

One response by the regulators was to allow an increasing variety of time deposits, thus adding a type of quantity control through the imposition of minimum maturities. Ceiling rates for certificates were usually raised by creating a new type of account with a longer term. In 1966, all certificates with an original maturity of six months or more were treated alike. By the late 1970s, there were different ceilings for a variety of certificates with terms extending up to eight years. (Figure 1-1 shows the highest rate permitted for any certificate as of a given date.) These long-term certificates may be seen as a concession to the viability of thrifts and the housing industry, as they provided a better match with the thrifts' long-term fixed-rate mortgage loans and weakened the impact of monetary policy. Longer maturities had to carry higher interest rates, however, so the added stability of deposits was gained at a price. Between 1973 and 1975, the quantity of time deposits remained virtually unchanged; in 1973, however, nearly all of these accounts were earning less than 6 percent, whereas in 1975 nearly all were above 6 percent (see figure 1-2).

The existing control structure, intended to assure solvency and to promote residential construction, instead discriminated against savers and limited the availability of mortgage financing. These regulations began to be circumvented through the use of innovative financial instruments by both the traditional depository institutions and their new competitors.

This process of innovation and change raised several policy issues. Monetary policy became less effective as the availability of market-rate deposit

---

8. Disintermediation is the withdrawal of funds from financial intermediaries such as thrift institutions. Ibid.; and Hendershott and Villani, *Regulation and Reform of the Housing Finance System*, pp. 55–66.

instruments reduced the effects of credit restraint on the ability to attract new funds. The viability of thrift institutions was threatened, however, because of their dependence on short-term investments to fund long-term assets in a period when short-term interest rates remained above the return on long-term assets. And the fate of the housing industry depended on the health of the thrift institutions. Finally, the widening gap between deposit rate ceilings and market rates of interest seemed increasingly unfair to small savers.

Government response was initially schizophrenic, as seen in the unsuccessful efforts to reform regulation during the 1970s. The Hunt commission was appointed by the president in 1970 to "review and study the structure, operation, and regulation of the private financial institutions in the United States, for the purpose of formulating recommendations that would improve the functioning of the private financial system."[9] Its report urged lifting deposit rate ceilings but called for the continued prohibition against the payment of interest on demand deposits. The members also recommended uniform tax and regulatory treatment of all depository institutions.[10] Their deregulatory inclinations stopped short of complete decontrol, however; they failed to endorse interstate banking and business deposits at thrift institutions. By the time the commission issued its report, however, the financial strains in the economy had eased, lessening the impetus for reform.

In 1975, the Senate passed the Financial Institutions Act (S. 1267), embodying many of the recommendations of the Hunt commission, but the legislation did not advance in the House. Thrifts were not persuaded that they could survive without rate ceilings and in direct competition with banks. These concerns were given greater weight in Congress's FINE study.[11] By 1977, legislation had been reintroduced to reform the regulation of banks and thrift institutions. Agreement, however, was still lacking. Some of the proposed regulatory changes promoted competition among

9. *The Report of the President's Commission on Financial Structure and Regulation* (Government Printing Office, 1971), p. 1.

10. Ibid., pp. 23–29, 31–75, 87–95. See also commentaries on the commission's report by George J. Benston, Dwight M. Jaffee, Sam Peltzman, and Allan H. Meltzer in *Journal of Money, Credit, and Banking*, vol. 4 (November 1972), pp. 985–1009.

11. *Financial Institutions and the Nation's Economy (FINE)*, Hearings before the Subcommittee on Financial Institutions Supervision, Regulation and Insurance of the House Committee on Banking, Currency and Housing, 94 Cong. 1 and 2 sess. (GPO, 1976). See also Donald Hester, "Special Interests: The FINE Situation," *Journal of Money, Credit, and Banking*, vol. 9 (November 1977), pp. 652–61.

institutions while others sought to preserve the traditional isolation of individual markets.

Events began to outpace congressional actions. In early 1978, the Federal Reserve Board and Federal Deposit Insurance Corporation authorized commercial banks to offer automatic transfer (ATS) accounts, a system for using savings accounts as checking accounts, thereby breaching the federal prohibition on payment of interest on demand deposits. Shortly thereafter, the courts overturned the decision, but gave Congress until 1980 to validate the original ATS authorization.

In the face of substantial disintermediation during the interest rate rise of 1978, a new instrument—the money market certificate—was authorized for all depository institutions. It carried an interest rate linked to the six-month Treasury bill discount rate, was offered at a six-month maturity, and required a $10,000 minimum deposit. Because market rates rose above the old rate ceilings, this certificate, and the thirty-month "small savers certificate" authorized since 1980, became extremely popular, while passbook and fixed-rate certificate accounts declined in importance (see figure 1-2). Nevertheless, the ceilings are still binding on $207 billion in old fixed-rate certificates earning 6 to 8 percent and on $335 billion in regular (passbook savings) accounts at all depository institutions.[12] And the 5.25 percent ceiling on $72 billion in interest-bearing transaction accounts[13] is also below market rates.

Market-rate instruments are most important for those institutions relying on household deposits; the money market and small savers certificates now represent more than a third of the liabilities of savings and loans, a similar fraction for mutual savings banks, and more than one-fourth of the liabilities of small commercial banks.[14] Jumbo certificates (those issued in denominations of $100,000 or more and sold primarily to institutional investors) also carry market rates of interest, and they too account for an increasing share of thrifts' liabilities. The growth of these market-linked certificates lessened the impact of interest rate ceilings on the quantity of

12. Data are as of the end of September 1981. Author's calculations based on Federal Reserve Board, *Statistical Release H.6* (October 16, 1981), p. 4, and subsequent issues; and FHLBB, "Savings and Loan Activity in September," October 30, 1981.

13. Federal Reserve Board, *Statistical Release H.6*.

14. Small commercial banks are those with less than $100 million in assets. Author's calculations based on Edward C. Ettin, "Petitions for Ceiling Rate Adjustments and Strategies for Deregulation," memorandum to the Depository Institutions Deregulation Committee (March 18, 1981), pp. A11–14.

savings flowing to depository institutions, but raised the average cost of funds to the institutions.

This substantial deregulation of institutions' short-term liabilities was not accompanied by a corresponding relaxation of restrictions on long-term liabilities and on assets.[15] In particular, deposit liabilities became highly sensitive to market interest rates, yet most thrifts were not permitted to offer variable-rate mortgages (loans with interest rates that adjust to changes in market rates). Rate ceilings and asset restrictions were ultimately viewed as hindrances to the thrifts' competitive position; in addition, they no longer achieved their original objectives of promoting saving and residential construction. In 1979, while responding to the need to make a decision on ATS, Congress attempted to effect a wide-ranging reform of the industry, although the two houses initially could not agree on a timetable or a structure for deregulation. The Depository Institutions Deregulation and Monetary Control Act of 1980 was eventually rushed through Congress as interest rates rose to record levels in February and March of that year.[16]

The act supersedes the authority of the individual federal and state regulatory bodies in many respects. It permits thrift institutions to expand their asset powers by writing consumer loans, issuing credit cards, holding corporate debt, and becoming more involved with service corporations. All depository institutions may now offer interest-bearing transaction accounts (often called NOW accounts). The act established the Depository Institutions Deregulation Committee (DIDC) to oversee the lifting of deposit rate ceilings during a six-year transition period. The authority of the Federal Reserve Board to impose reserve requirements[17] on all classes of transaction accounts and all nonpersonal time deposits was extended to include thrift institutions and nonmember banks. All depository institutions offering transaction accounts have access to the Federal Reserve discount window and to check clearing and other services, although such processing is no longer provided free of charge.

It was anticipated that the changes would be implemented in a "grad-

15. Contrast the new certificates with the earlier practice of setting the highest rates on the longest-term accounts.

16. See Kenneth A. McLean, "Legislative Background of the Depository Institutions Deregulation and Monetary Control Act of 1980" in *Savings and Loan Asset Management Under Deregulation, Proceedings of the Sixth Annual Conference* (Federal Home Loan Bank of San Francisco, 1980), pp. 16–30.

17. Reserve requirements compel depository institutions to maintain vault cash or deposits at the Federal Reserve equal to a percentage of their more liquid liabilities.

ual," "orderly" manner, and "as rapidly as economic conditions warrant."[18] Renewed disruptions during 1980 and 1981, however, made it apparent that deregulation was not a panacea. But neither was deregulation the cause of the ills experienced by investors, borrowers, and institutions. Rather, the operating losses, the housing slump, and the threats of institutional failure resulted from the confluence of adverse economic conditions and the partial deregulation and incomplete adjustment of financial markets and institutions.

Condition of the Thrift Industry

The spread between mortgage interest rates and regulated deposit rates gave thrift institutions a comfortable operating margin during most of the late 1960s and the 1970s. Bank competition for deposits was limited by rate ceilings below those of the thrifts, and banks lacked the tax incentives and regulatory constraints to compete for mortgage loans. And the regulatory agencies restricted competition among thrifts through a conservative merger and expansion policy. Hence there was little pressure on profit margins.

In recent years, however, the profitability of the thrifts has fallen substantially, as shown in table 1-1. Savings and loan associations' return on average assets was only 0.14 percent for 1980, down from 0.84 percent in 1978. Mutual savings banks had a loss equal to 0.12 percent of average assets in 1980, compared with typical profits well in excess of 0.30 percent of assets.

Credit unions have experienced periods of lower earnings as well, but the maturities of their assets and liabilities are more closely matched than are those of the mortgage-lending institutions, so they can adjust more readily to changes in returns on loans and deposits. They have been adversely affected by the rise in interest rates in another way, however, in which government regulation is again a factor. Interest ceilings on deposits have slowed the inflow of funds at the same time that rate ceilings on consumer loans have reduced profits. Because credit unions are restricted by the "common bond" provisions to a single group of employees, they are more limited than other financial intermediaries in the sources of their funds, and they have suffered some liquidity problems as a result. Higher rates of

18. See section 204 of the Depository Institutions Deregulation and Monetary Control Act of 1980, 94 Stat. 143.

Table 1-1. *Profitability of the Thrift Institutions, 1961–81*

Retained earnings as percent of average total assets

Year	Savings and loan associations[a]	Mutual savings banks	Credit unions
1961–65	0.80	0.45	0.78
1966–70	0.56	0.30	0.77
1971–75	0.65	0.47	0.66
1976	0.64	0.45	0.63
1977	0.79	0.55	0.55
1978	0.84	0.58	0.36
1979	0.68	0.46	0.30
1980	0.14	−0.12	0.42
1981[b]	−0.49	−0.64	n.a.

Sources: National Association of Mutual Savings Banks, *1981 National Fact Book of Mutual Savings Banking* (New York: NAMSB, 1981), p. 39; NAMSB, "Research Analysis of Monthly Savings Bank Trends," August 25, 1981, p. 6; Federal Home Loan Bank Board, news release, September 29, 1981; Credit Union National Association, *All Kinds of People: 1979 Yearbook* (Washington, D.C.: CUNA, 1979), p. 37; CUNA, *Credit Union Statistical Report 1980* (CUNA, 1981), p. 5.

n.a. Not available.

a. Data before 1976 is for Federal Savings and Loan Insurance Corporation-insured savings and loan associations; data after 1976 covers all savings and loan associations.

b. Estimate based on first six months' results at annual rate.

unemployment and slower growth in real wages have been concentrated in those areas and industries where credit unions are most prevalent. Loan delinquencies have risen for some credit unions. In general, however, this industry's difficulties may be characterized as stagnation rather than decline. Therefore, as both the type and magnitude of difficulties are fundamentally different from those of the savings and loan associations and the mutual savings banks, credit unions will be excluded from all subsequent discussion of thrift institutions in this study.

These adverse conditions in the thrift industry are largely due to government policy decisions of the 1960s and before. Tax laws and regulatory practice have forced savings and loans and mutual savings banks to hold fixed-rate long-term residential mortgages as their principal assets and to accept the short-term deposits of households as their major source of funds (liabilities). By the end of 1980, mortgage loans accounted for 79.8 percent of savings and loan association assets and 59.0 percent of mutual savings bank assets.[19] Thrift institutions hold 40 percent of the outstanding mortgage debt and originate 49 percent of mortgages written.[20]

19. FHLBB, "Savings and Loan Activity in July"; Federal Deposit Insurance Corporation, *1980 Annual Report* (FDIC, 1981), p. 250.

20. NAMSB, *1981 National Fact Book*, p. 50; U.S. Department of Housing and Urban Development, *1979 Statistical Yearbook* (GPO, 1980), pp. 257–58.

Regulations limited the ways in which the thrifts could dispose of their profits other than plowing them back into mortgages. The minority with stock forms of ownership could pay higher dividends to shareholders. All put large sums into contingency reserves, both for security and to escape taxation. The balance was used to compensate bank officers and, more important, to increase deposits by providing enhanced service. Thrift institutions developed extensive and costly branch networks, expanded their hours of operation, and offered certain amenities (such as private club membership) to their customers. Such expenditures often were not consistent with the volume of business attracted. Studies of thrift institutions have therefore found high expense ratios for the smallest firms and a tendency for all firms to provide more service than would be demanded in the absence of deposit rate regulation.[21] Figure 1-3 shows that expenses of thrift institutions increased sharply after 1966 as rate ceilings became binding, offsetting the trend to lower costs that came with productivity gains and increasing firm size.[22] Nonprice competition (in the form of more service) thus replaced price competition (in the form of higher interest rates).

The system worked as long as the return on assets exceeded the cost of liabilities by a sufficient margin to cover expenses. What has happened, however, is that interest rates have risen sharply, and the liabilities of thrift institutions—because they are short-term instruments—have adjusted to the new level of rates more quickly than have the asset portfolios (see table 1-2). To compound the problem, the spread between short-term and long-term rates virtually disappeared after mid-1980.[23] There was no margin between short-term deposits and long-term loans with which to pay operating costs, thus leaving loan origination fees (service charges paid by new borrowers) as the primary source of short-run profits on newly written mortgages.

21. See Robert A. Taggart, Jr., "Effects of Deposit Rate Ceilings," *Journal of Money, Credit, and Banking,* vol. 10 (May 1978), pp. 139–57; Robert A. Taggart and Geoffrey Woglom, "Savings Bank Reactions to Rate Ceilings and Rising Market Rates," *New England Economic Review* (Federal Reserve Bank of Boston, September–October 1978), pp. 17–31; James E. McNulty, "Economies of Scale in the S&L Industry: New Evidence and Implications for Profitability," *Federal Home Loan Bank Board Journal,* vol. 14 (February 1981), pp. 2–8.

22. The ratio of expenses to assets is a reliable indicator of performance. The more commonly cited ratio—expenses to gross income—is misleading because rising interest rates decrease the expense ratio although they do not alter the cost of processing transactions.

23. These two effects may be described respectively as an upward shift and a flattening (or inversion) of the interest rate yield curve.

Figure 1-3. *Operating Expense Performance of Thrift Institutions, 1951–80*

Operating expenses as a share of average assets (percent)

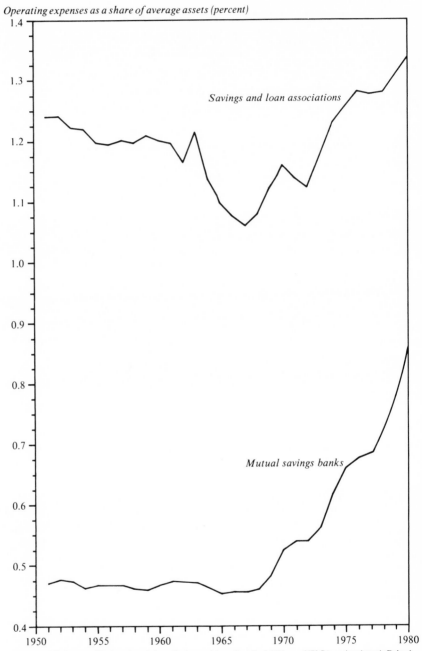

Sources: U. S. League of Savings Associations, *Savings and Loan Fact Book* (Chicago: USLSA, various issues); Federal Deposit Insurance Corporation, *Annual Report* (FDIC, various issues).

Table 1-2. *Inflation and Selected Interest Rates, 1961–80*

Percent

Year	Inflation rate[a]	Interest rate[b]	Return on assets[c]	Rate paid on liabilities[d]
1961	0.9	2.97	n.a.	3.90
1962	1.8	3.26	n.a.	4.08
1963	1.5	3.55	n.a.	4.17
1964	1.5	3.97	n.a.	4.18
1965	2.2	4.38	5.93	4.25
1966	3.2	5.55	5.94	4.53
1967	3.0	5.10	6.01	4.72
1968	4.4	5.90	6.13	4.74
1969	5.1	7.83	6.32	4.89
1970	5.4	7.72	6.56	5.30
1971	5.0	5.11	6.81	5.38
1972	4.2	4.69	6.98	5.41
1973	5.7	8.15	7.16	5.60
1974	8.7	9.87	7.43	6.14
1975	9.3	6.33	7.66	6.32
1976	5.2	5.35	7.95	6.38
1977	5.8	5.60	8.21	6.44
1978	7.3	7.99	8.47	6.67
1979	8.5	10.91	8.83	7.47
1980	9.0	12.29	9.31	8.94

Sources: *Economic Report of the President, 1981*, pp. 237, 308; Federal Home Loan Bank Board, *Savings and Home Financing Source Book, 1979* (July 1980), pp. 59–61; FHLBB, unpublished data (1981).

n.a. Not available.

a. Implicit price deflator for gross national product, percentage change over previous year.

b. Prime commercial paper, four to six months, for 1961–November 1979; six-month paper beginning November 1979.

c. Average interest return on mortgages, insured savings associations.

d. Average effective dividend rate paid, Federal Home Loan Bank system members, 1961–64; average cost of funds, insured savings associations, 1965–80.

Although all depository institutions perform similar functions, they have not been equally affected by the rise in interest rates. Commercial banks hold a substantially smaller share of their assets in long-term fixed-rate investments, and this is true even of those small banks that serve as the principal mortgage lenders in rural areas. Real estate loans accounted for 17.1 percent of commercial banks' assets at the end of 1980, and the share was only slightly higher for small banks—21.5 percent for those with assets of $50 million to $99.9 million.[24] So policies addressing the thrift industry's asset inflexibility need not affect the operations of commercial banks.

24. FDIC, *Annual Report*, p. 265. Small commercial banks are heavily committed to financing farm production, however, which introduces an element of uncertainty in their assets. These loans, which account for 15 percent of the assets of the smallest banks, are usually secured by the farmers' anticipated production and thus are more susceptible to unexpected price changes than are real estate loans.

Figure 1-4. *Structure of Liabilities at Depository Institutions, December 1980*

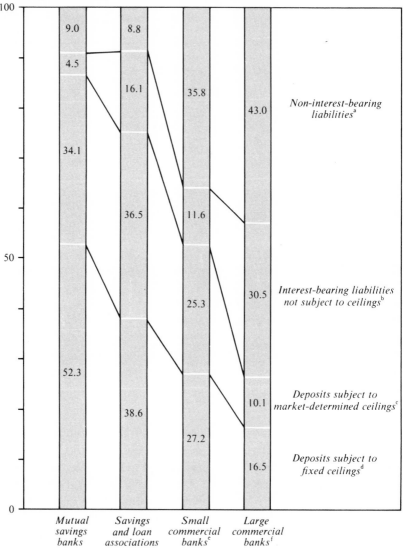

Percent of total liabilities

Source: Author's estimates based on Edward C. Ettin, "Petitions for Ceiling Rate Adjustments and Strategies for Deregulation," memorandum to the Depository Institutions Deregulation Committee (March 18, 1981), pp. A11–A14.
a. Demand deposits, other liabilities, capital, surplus, and other reserve accounts.
b. Jumbo certificates, other borrowings, and funds advanced from foreign offices.
c. Money market certificates and small savers certificates.
d. Passbook accounts, NOW accounts, and fixed-ceiling time deposits.
e. Banks with less than $100 million in assets.
f. Banks with $100 million or more in assets. Data are for domestic offices only.

Table 1-3. *Interest Rates on New and Existing Mortgages, 1965–81*
Percent

| Year | Rate on new mortgages[a] | Average return on existing mortgages | |
		FSLIC-insured savings and loan associations	Mutual savings banks
1965–70	7.23	6.19	5.60
1971–75	8.28	7.21	6.74
1976	9.11	7.95	7.38
1977	9.02	8.21	7.61
1978	9.58	8.47	7.92
1979	10.92	8.83	8.26
1980	12.95	9.31	8.64
1981[b]	14.37	9.72	9.34

Sources: FHLBB, *Savings and Home Financing Source Book, 1979*, tables 34, 39; FHLBB, "Mortgage Rates at New Highs in Early June," July 7, 1981, table 2; NAMSB, *1981 National Fact Book*, p. 39; FHLBB, news release, September 29, 1981.
a. Effective interest rate on conventional first-mortgage loans originated by all major types of lenders for the purchase of previously occupied single-family homes.
b. Estimate based on first six months' results.

Although there are differences in the composition of assets between banks and thrift institutions, the liabilities of small commercial banks do bear a strong resemblance to those of the thrift institutions. Both are dependent on consumer deposits (as shown in figure 1-4), and thus face the dilemma of meeting the rising cost of funds or losing accounts as deposit rate controls become less binding. Regulations affecting deposit rates must therefore take account of small commercial banks' interests. But small banks and large banks are indistinguishable in law, so any action to aid thrifts and small banks usually benefits large banks as well.

Rates on new mortgages did not change very rapidly until the late 1960s. Thus the average and marginal rates of return on thrift institutions' mortgage portfolios were roughly equal. After 1966, however, mortgage interest rates began to rise. As shown in table 1-3, the average return on mortgage assets rose too, but more slowly, reflecting the preponderance in the portfolios of previously written mortgages still carrying the earlier low interest rates.

A calculation showing an asset earning less than the market rate of return for equivalent instruments cannot, by definition, be based on the market value of the asset. In the capital markets, where assets are traded on an auction basis, prices of fixed-rate instruments vary with fluctuations in interest rates and according to maturity. For example, a $1,000 bond with five years to maturity paying $150 per year (a coupon rate of 15 percent) is worth more than another $1,000 five-year bond paying $100 per year (a coupon rate of 10 percent). If the market interest rate for new five-year bonds is 15 percent, the first bond would sell at par ($1,000), but the market value of the second bond would be approximately $832. Mortgages held by thrift institutions, however, are usually reported at book value—the original par value of the loans reduced by the amount mortgagors have paid on the principal. Therefore, saying that assets are earning below-market rates of return is equivalent to saying that the market value of these assets has been reduced to the point at which the interest payments equal market rates.

The magnitude of the unrealized capital loss on the mortgage portfolios of thrift institutions can be estimated. Using industry averages for maturity, turnover, average return, and rates on new mortgages, the market value of assets can be compared with the book value.[25] Deposit rate ceilings have similarly depressed the market value of thrift institution liabilities.[26] Because deposits have much shorter maturities and frequently carry market rates of return, however, the reduction in market value is not nearly as great as on the asset side of the balance sheet. The market values of assets, liabilities, and net worth are shown in table 1-4.

Calculations based on the table show that the gap between the book value and market value of mortgages (assets) widened markedly from 1978 on: it jumped from $14.8 billion in 1977 to $26.4 billion in 1978, and then increased to $49.2 billion in 1979 and $84.9 billion in 1980. This steep increase was a reflection of the rapid rise in mortgage interest rates starting in 1978, shown in table 1-3. By mid-year 1981, if the mortgages held by thrift institutions had been liquidated, they would have realized $111.2 billion less than the value at which they were carried on the books. This amount is a transfer of wealth from the institutions to homeowners holding low-rate mortgages. If the deposit liabilities had been similarly sold at a

25. See Richard W. Kopcke and Geoffrey R. H. Woglom, "Regulation Q and Savings Bank Solvency—The Connecticut Experience," in *The Regulation of Financial Institutions*, Conference Series No. 21, *Proceedings of a Conference Sponsored by the Federal Reserve Bank of Boston and the National Science Foundation*, October 1979 (Federal Reserve Bank of Boston, 1980), pp. 68–95; and Richard W. Kopcke, "The Condition of Massachusetts Savings Banks and California Savings and Loan Associations," in *The Future of the Thrift Industry*, Conference Series No. 24, *Proceedings of a Conference Sponsored by the Federal Reserve Bank of Boston*, October 1981 (Federal Reserve Bank of Boston, forthcoming).

26. See David H. Pyle, "The Losses on Savings Deposits from Interest Rate Regulation," *Bell Journal of Economics and Management Science*, vol. 5 (Autumn 1974), pp. 614–22.

Table 1-4. *Book Value and Market Value of Assets, Liabilities, and Net Worth of Thrift Institutions, 1970–81*[a]

Billions of dollars

	Assets		Liabilities		Net worth	
End of year	*Book value*	*Market value*	*Book value*	*Market value*	*Book value*	*Market value*
1970	255.2	244.6	237.1	235.4	18.1	9.2
1971	295.6	289.0	275.7	276.0	19.9	13.0
1972	343.7	337.1	321.5	320.4	22.2	16.7
1973	378.6	366.5	353.9	350.4	24.6	16.1
1974	405.1	388.9	378.7	375.1	26.4	13.8
1975	459.3	444.3	431.1	429.1	28.2	15.2
1976	526.7	513.7	495.7	495.8	31.1	17.8
1977	606.5	591.7	571.4	568.3	35.2	23.4
1978	681.7	655.3	641.8	632.8	40.0	22.5
1979	742.4	693.2	698.2	685.6	44.2	7.6
1980	801.4	716.5	756.7	734.0	44.7	−17.5
1981[b]	821.1	709.9	778.7	754.0	42.4	−44.1

Sources: Author's calculations based on FHLBB, *Savings and Home Financing Source Book, 1979*, tables 3A, 7, 34, 38; FHLBB, "Savings and Loan Activity in July," August 28, 1981, table 3; NAMSB, *1981 National Fact Book*, p. 10; NAMSB, "Research Analysis of Monthly Savings Bank Trends," August 25, 1981, table 2. Figures are rounded.

a. All savings and loan associations and mutual savings banks.

b. As of June 30, 1981.

discount to reflect their market value, they would have brought $24.7 billion less than their book value. And this gain for the thrift institutions is the amount of the loss incurred by depositors who have their savings in passbook and low-rate certificate accounts. As of mid-year 1981, therefore, there had been a net transfer of $86.5 billion from the thrift industry to the household sector. This net transfer is equal to the difference between book value and market value of net worth.

This does not mean that the thrift industry as a whole is not viable, or that firms will be unable to meet their payrolls and their other financial obligations. Rather, the import of this calculation is that at current interest rate levels the thrift institutions' earnings will remain depressed. Investment income depends on the market value of assets, while interest expense is a function of the level of liabilities. Net earnings are therefore related to the market value of net worth.

It is not appropriate to use the (negative) market-value net worth as an estimate of the amount payable to depositors by the Federal Savings and Loan Insurance Corporation and the Federal Deposit Insurance Corporation. The deposit insurance funds do face a much greater exposure to loss

Table 1-5. *Factors Affecting Market-Value Calculations*

Year	Refinancing gap[a] (percentage points)	New residential construction (thousands of starts per year)	Mortgage turnover[b] (percent)
1961–65	0.98[c]	1,512.6	15.3
1966–70	1.04	1,406.3	10.9
1971–75	1.07	1,808.9	12.0
1976	1.16	1,547.6	12.7
1977	0.81	1,989.8	14.0
1978	1.11	2,023.3	13.1
1979	2.09	1,749.1	11.1
1980	3.64	1,298.5	8.4
1981[d]	5.17	1,282.5	6.7

Sources: Author's calculations based on FHLBB, *Savings and Home Financing Source Book, 1979*, tables 7, 14, 34, 39; *Economic Report of the President, 1981*, p. 284; U.S. Department of Commerce, *Survey of Current Business*, vol. 61 (June 1981), p. 58; FHLBB, "Savings and Loan Activity in July," August 28, 1981; FHLBB, "Mortgage Interest Rates at New High in Early June"; FHLBB, news release, September 29, 1981.
  a. Difference between interest rates on conventional first mortgage loans for purchase of previously occupied single-family homes and average return on mortgages held by insured savings and loan associations.
  b. Mortgage loans repaid as a share of average mortgage loans held at insured savings and loan associations. Excludes sales and purchases of mortgages and participations.
  c. Estimate.
  d. Estimate based on first six months' results.

than ever before, but liquidation of the entire industry is a purely theoretical exercise. Thus, while the potential for serious difficulties exists, these estimates do not serve as a guide to the costs of recovery. They do, however, provide evidence of the deterioration of the industry's financial condition.

Market-value calculations are sensitive to a number of factors. Mortgage turnover is one variable. When a home is sold, the existing mortgage may be assumed by the new owner or paid off by the old. Many contracts permit the lender to demand payment upon sale, thereby preventing assumption, although the legality of this provision is being challenged.[27] (Congress is considering legislation to uphold the right of lenders to enforce the due-on-sale provision in mortgages.) As interest rates have risen, the rate of turnover has declined, especially among the low-rate mortgages that represent the greatest potential loss for thrifts (see table 1-5). Homeowners are unwilling or unable to sell houses carrying a nonassumable low-rate mortgage. As the table also shows, there has been a slowing in new residential construction because of the higher cost of new mortgages. Thrifts have thus been denied the increases in average portfolio yields that would come from writing mortgages on large numbers of new homes.

27. See *Business Week* (May 25, 1981), p. 128.

Higher rates of mortgage turnover and home building in the future would raise the industry's market value of assets. If interest rates drop over the next few years, both would be expected to accelerate. The calculations above assume rates of turnover and construction higher than that recently experienced, but below what might be anticipated in a resurgence of the housing industry. The market rate of interest itself is another factor in the market-value calculation. With a fall in rates, the thrift industry's apparent loss of net worth would be rapidly reversed.

Residential mortgages do have one important virtue as an asset. They are particularly well secured in an environment of rapidly rising property values. Mortgage insurance, provided through the government or by private firms, further lessens the default risk to the mortgagee. Institutions do experience a higher rate of delinquencies and foreclosures during an economic downturn. The delinquent loan ratio at savings and loan associations averaged 1.22 percent in the first half of 1981, up from 0.90 percent in the first half of 1979 but still well below the 1.52 percent rate during the first half of 1976.[28] Cash flow can be depressed until payments become current or until the foreclosed property is sold. Solvency of the thrift institution in these cases is usually not a concern. Interest rate risk is thus the only important uncertainty in holding a portfolio of fixed-rate residential mortgages.

The Liquidity Issue

Solvency and liquidity are the two principal concerns of a depository institution during a time of slow growth and depressed earnings. A firm is considered solvent if the book value of its assets is at least equal to that of its liabilities. This is an accounting concept useful in assessing the general health of an institution and its long-term viability, but the question of solvency has little impact on the day-to-day functioning of a financial institution. As has been shown, the thrift industry may be technically insolvent, yet its thousands of firms continue to transact business and serve customers. Deep or prolonged insolvency can lead to the failure of a firm, but the more immediate concern is that of liquidity. That is the ability of a firm to meet its payment obligations in a timely fashion with cash and other liquid assets on hand.

28. FHLBB, *Savings and Home Financing Source Book, 1979* (July 1980), p. 52; FHLBB, "Savings and Loan Activity in July."

Thrift institutions remain liquid by balancing cash outlays with cash receipts. Inflows derive from new deposits, principal and interest payments on mortgages and other loans, and new borrowing. Outlays are required for withdrawals of deposit principal and interest, employee compensation and other operating expenses, interest payable on borrowed funds and repayments of borrowing, and disbursements for new loans made. Interest credited to an account remaining on deposit has no net effect on cash flow. Some of these items, such as mortgage repayments and employee compensation, are contractual and thus relatively predictable and insensitive to changing economic conditions. The firm itself has control over the amount of new loans made, while it is vulnerable to withdrawals largely at the discretion of depositors.

The loosening of restrictions on deposit rate ceilings has been only partially successful in stemming savings outflows. On balance, there was a small net inflow of new money ($10.7 billion) to savings and loans during 1980, with a sharp reversal in the first half of 1981; withdrawals exceeded deposits by $11.1 billion during this latter period, with more than half of the loss coming in the month of June. The 1981 rate of withdrawals represents 4.3 percent of deposits at an annual rate.[29] Mutual savings banks have suffered deposit outflows almost continuously since 1978. Net withdrawals totaled $4.8 billion in all of 1980 and $6.2 billion (8.2 percent of deposits at an annual rate) in the first six months of 1981.[30] The lack of new deposits is a departure from earlier experience. During the 1970s, annual net new deposits averaged 7.4 percent of total deposits at savings and loans and 1.3 percent at mutual savings banks.[31]

In a time of operating losses, increases in deposits are an important factor in maintaining sufficient liquidity. Unless the cash inflow exceeds the shortfall between income and expense, the institution may be forced to liquidate its assets—at a loss—to meet deposit and interest withdrawals and repayments due lenders. Institutions have resorted to increased borrowing as one method of covering their obligations and avoiding the sale of assets. At the end of June 1981, advances from the Federal Home Loan Bank System and other borrowing amounted to 12.2 percent of liabilities at savings and loan associations. Borrowing reached 9 percent of liabilities for

29. FHLBB, "Savings and Loan Activity in July," and "Savings and Loan Activity in June," July 28, 1981.
30. NAMSB, "Research Analysis of Monthly Savings Bank Trends," August 25, 1981.
31. FHLBB, *Savings and Home Financing Source Book, 1979*, pp. 9, 18; NAMSB, *1981 National Fact Book*, pp. 17, 23.

the first time at the end of 1974, fell to lower levels in the late 1970s, then rose above 10 percent at the end of 1979.[32] Most mutual savings banks do not have access to a special lending facility such as the Federal Home Loan Banks. They have been even less successful than the savings and loans in maintaining the level of their assets. Nondeposit liabilities of mutual savings banks were 5.3 percent of liabilities at the end of June 1981, compared with the previous high of 3.9 percent at the end of 1979.[33] Such borrowing is intended to cover cyclical shifts in deposit and mortgage flows.

Insufficient liquidity would present a thrift institution and its regulators with a difficult choice. Additional loans could be provided to meet a temporary difficulty, but that course of action implies an added expense for the high interest rates these loans carry. In the presence of technical insolvency more borrowing might be imprudent. The institution would be helped by direct cash grants, although that plan would face the same objections. Ultimately, an illiquid institution could be forced to merge into a healthier firm, with the deposit insuror providing cash assistance to the acquiring firm. The only other alternative is to allow the institution to default, but that would lead so directly to a run on deposits—which the insurance agencies are pledged to support—that the regulators would not permit a default to occur. The FSLIC and FDIC can themselves take over and operate a thrift institution in danger of default.

How likely is the prospect of widespread liquidity crises in the thrift industry? Table 1-6 illustrates the cash flow situation for the savings and loan industry. Payments of interest and principal on mortgage loans generate strong cash inflows. Discretionary prepayments and loan liquidations slowed during the first half of 1980 and again in 1981 as rising interest rates retarded home purchase activity and increased the use of mortgage assumption and other creative financing techniques. Nevertheless, required amortizations and interest payments will continue as important sources of liquid funds regardless of economic conditions. Other sources of cash included sales of loans and securities in the first half of 1980 and increased borrowing thereafter. Deposit growth for the eighteen-month period as a whole was slightly negative. Associations continued to make new mortgage loans at a rate exceeding repayments, particularly during the period of

32. FHLBB, "Savings and Loan Activity in July"; and FHLBB, *Savings and Home Financing Source Book, 1979*, p. 6.
33. NAMSB, "Research Analysis," table 2; NAMSB, *1981 National Fact Book*, p. 10.

Table 1-6. *Cash Flow Analysis for FSLIC-Insured Savings and Loan Associations, January 1980–June 1981*

Billions of dollars

Cash item	January–June 1980	July–December 1980	January–June 1981
Cash flow activity			
Contractual payments and receipts			
Mortgage loans repaid	17.5	23.2	16.9
Mortgage interest	21.6	22.8	24.0
Other income	6.8	7.0	7.0
Interest on borrowed money	−2.9	−3.1	−4.1
Interest on jumbo certificates	−2.2	−2.5	−3.3
Other interest paid out	−4.7	−4.9	−5.1
Operating expenses	−3.8	−4.0	−4.2
Total	32.3	38.5	31.2
Deposit activity			
New deposits received	204.3	219.8	222.9
New deposits withdrawn	−202.0	−211.5	−234.0
Total	2.3	8.3	−11.1
Association activity			
Net loan sales	2.2	0.7	0.4
Mortgage loans closed	−25.7	−45.6	−29.7
Increase (decrease) in borrowing	−0.4	9.6	10.2
Total	−23.9	−35.3	−19.1
Summary			
Contractual payments	32.3	38.5	31.2
Deposit activity	2.3	8.3	−11.1
Association activity	−23.9	−35.3	−19.1
Net cash flow	10.7	11.5	1.0
Resources and exposure			
Resources (end of period)			
Excess cash and securities[a]	27.3	31.2	30.9
Mortgage-backed securities[a]	22.3	27.0	29.6
Total[a]	49.6	58.2	60.5
Exposure (end of period)			
Private borrowing	−13.9	−17.1	−20.5
Noninsured jumbo certificates	−16.9	−20.0	−21.7
Provision for other withdrawals	. . .	−11.1	−11.1[b]
Total	−30.8	−48.2	−53.3
Cash position summary			
Net cash flow	10.7	11.5	1.0
Resources	49.6	58.2	60.5
Exposure	−30.8	−48.2	−53.3
Net cash position	29.5	21.5	8.2

Source: Estimates based on FHLBB, "Savings and Loan Activity in July"; "Savings and Loan Activity in June," July 28, 1981; and "Savings and Loan Activity in December," January 30, 1981.

a. Cash and securities in excess of regulatory minimum. Securities at book value; market value is less.

b. January–June rate of withdrawals. January–March withdrawals were at $1.3 billion semiannual rate; April–June withdrawal rate was $20.9 billion.

lower interest rates in 1980. The net effect of these flows was a moderate cash surplus for 1980 and only a very small surplus in the first half of 1981.

A crude evaluation of the liquidity position of the industry can be made by combining the net cash flow with potential new cash claims and available resources. The bottom part of the table shows the results of this exercise. Since it can be assumed that funds borrowed from private institutions (that is, other than Federal Home Loan Banks), the uninsured portion of jumbo certificates, and certain other deposits are vulnerable to withdrawals, a declining liquidity position is the result. If the rate of deposit loss remains at the high levels of the April–June 1981 period, the $8.2 billion margin indicated in the last line of the table could turn negative by the end of 1981.[34]

Deposit losses at mutual savings banks contributed to a slight negative cash flow during the first six months of 1981. The cash drain was minimized by a very conservative policy on making new loans and by an increase in borrowing. Despite the outflow, however, savings banks have a high proportion of assets in liquid form and thus are in a more stable liquidity position than are the savings and loans. Cash and securities (excluding loans) were 31 percent of savings bank assets in mid-1981, compared with 14 percent for savings and loan associations.[35] As a group, the mutual savings banks are unlikely to encounter severe liquidity problems under any plausible economic scenario.

All institutions are not average, however, and there is likely to be a problem of illiquidity at a small number of institutions. Some mutual savings banks, for example, have a large share of assets in long-term bonds. These instruments have the same low yield as old mortgages but lack amortization of principal and the possibility of prepayment. Some institutions therefore may suffer cash flow problems. The regulatory agencies would probably induce the merger or liquidation of any such institution that also had a large negative market-value net worth. Therefore, federal assistance to thrifts under existing programs in the next few years will probably be focused on those institutions unable to meet their short-term obligations,

34. In fact, deposit losses in the July–September 1981 quarter exceeded those of the April–June period. However, the introduction of the tax-exempt certificate on October 1 reversed this pattern. It remains to be seen whether this will be sufficient over the long run to avoid declining liquidity. FHLBB, "Savings and Loan Activity in September," p. 1 and table 1.

35. Data are for all mutual savings banks and FSLIC-insured savings and loan associations. NAMSB, "Research Analysis"; FHLBB, "Savings and Loan Activity in July," table 3.

while others in a better cash position (though perhaps technically insol-vent) will be allowed to remain in operation.

If thrift institutions avoid a liquidity crisis, it will be at the expense of the housing industry. The largest single discretionary item in an institution's cash flow account is the amount of new mortgage loans closed. This item is sensitive to the quantity of new deposits. Thrifts will seek to maintain a positive cash flow by reducing their mortgage-lending activity, investing instead in short-term liquid assets and sacrificing some income. Govern-ment programs already in place will be adequate for those institutions that encounter liquidity problems. An emphasis on new programs to improve liquidity may be viewed as policy for the housing industry rather than as a means of preventing thrift institution failures.

Chapter Two

Outlook for the Thrift Industry

The foregoing analysis has indicated the general magnitude of the problems faced by thrift institutions. In dealing exclusively with industry aggregates, however, important information is obscured. It is necessary to know the size and number of those firms that are in the weakest condition, the regions of the country in which they are located, and whether their problems are the result of low earnings, high costs, deposit outflows, mismanagement, or some combination of these. This chapter takes account of these factors and presents a forecast and analysis of the thrift institutions' difficulties for the next few years. On the basis of these findings, various policy alternatives will be evaluated in the concluding chapters of this study.

From a worrisome situation at the end of 1980, economic conditions turned even more sharply against the thrift institutions in 1981, as shown in table 2-1. The combination of high interest rates on deposits and weak deposit growth forced institutions to dip into their reserves in order to meet obligations to depositors, employees, and creditors. Net worth positions deteriorated. A continuation of these conditions would erode net worth at an increasing rate, as the base of earning assets would be depleted while liabilities would remain high. The level of net worth is an important determinant of the continued viability of a depository institution.

A more systematic approach to analyzing the financial condition of the thrift industry requires the use of data on individual firms and a model to relate the data in a consistent fashion. I developed such a model to forecast the income statements and balance sheets of thrift institutions.[1]

1. My forecasting model is based on accounting concepts and on the way capital markets function. A common set of interest rates prevails across geographic markets, and the market value of assets varies inversely with interest rates and increasing term to maturity. For the thrift industry, the high proportion of fixed-rate long-term residential mortgages limits the ability to change asset structure. Conversely, the maturities on the liability side are much shorter. Given an environment of interest rate volatility, these two observations imply that market values will fluctuate on the asset side (fixed rates) and that interest rates will vary relatively more on the liability side (fixed quantities).

The model takes existing (end of year 1980) asset portfolios and, using interest rate and

Table 2-1. *Economic Indicators, 1980–81*

Percent

Indicator	July–December 1980	January–June 1981
Interest rates		
Six-month Treasury bills	11.34	13.95
New mortgages	12.76	14.24
Deposit growth net of interest credited at thrift institutions,[a] annual rate	2.26	−5.30
Thrift institution[a] net income as a share of assets, annual rate	0.05	−0.52
Thrift institution[a] net worth as a share of assets (end of period)	5.58	5.16

Sources: *Federal Reserve Bulletin* (September 1980), tables 1 and 36, p. A27, and tables 1 and 35, p. A25 in January, March, and July 1981 issues; Federal Home Loan Bank Board, "Mortgage Interest Rates in Early July," August 4, 1981, table 2: FHLBB, "Savings and Loan Activity in July," August 28, 1981, tables 1 and 3, and "Savings and Loan Association Activity in May," June 26, 1981, tables 1 and 3; National Association of Mutual Savings Banks, "Research Analysis of Monthly Savings Bank Trends," April 24, 1981, and ibid., August 25, 1981; Federal Deposit Insurance Corporation, *1980 Annual Report* (FDIC, 1981), table 108.
a. FSLIC-insured savings and loan associations and all mutual savings banks.

The ultimate criterion of viability is whether there exists sufficient net worth to allow positive net income at some future time when the interest rate yield curve is normal, assets have been fully marked down to market value, and liabilities earn a market rate of return in a deregulated environment. This indicator of long-run viability can be used in conjunction with other criteria such as net worth ratios (net worth to assets or net worth to net income) and liquidity ratios (liquid assets to savings plus short-term borrowings) to assess the performance of the industry.

I developed three sets of interest rate assumptions. The first set corresponds to the administration's predictions for 1982 as reported in the mid-year budget review,[2] with less of a decline in rates than forecast by the administration for 1983; this is the most optimistic scenario. A pessimistic projection, which assumes a continuation of interest rates at mid-1981

---

turnover data, computes market value. It projects income based on old and new assets and estimates expenses based on historical operating costs and forecasts of interest rates. Liquidity shortages are resolved through increased borrowing.

Primary data for the calculations came from semiannual Federal Home Loan Bank Board tabulations on approximately 4,000 FSLIC-insured savings and loan associations and from quarterly FDIC reports on the approximately 320 mutual savings banks insured by that agency. Additional industrywide data on portfolio composition, interest rates, deposit growth, and deposit rate ceilings came from those same sources, as well as the Federal Reserve Board.

2. U.S. Office of Management and Budget, *Mid-Session Review of the 1982 Budget* (Government Printing Office, 1981), pp. 7, 69.

levels, represents the upper bound of the major private economic forecasters. The third scenario represents a point between these extremes, with a slow decline in short-term interest rates. All of the forecasts assume a continuation of existing deposit rate ceilings on certificates, an increase in the passbook rate from 5.5 percent in 1981 to 6.5 percent in 1983, and rates of deposit growth consistent with these ceilings and market interest rates. The effects of the tax-exempt (all savers) certificates created by the Economic Recovery Tax Act of 1981 are included.[3]

The results of this exercise are striking: the savings and loan industry will undergo a major restructuring as a result of large operating losses and the deterioration of net worth positions. At least one association in seven, and possibly more than one in four, will cease to exist as independent entities. Although voluntary mergers will be the primary instrument of this change, demands on the FSLIC insurance fund may strain its resources, requiring temporary assistance from the Treasury or the Federal Reserve System. By contrast, mutual savings banks will emerge from this difficult period largely intact. Their losses, though relatively greater than those of the savings and loans, will be turned back into profits more quickly. Any savings bank claims on the FDIC fund will be handled without aid from other agencies.

Savings and Loan Associations

Projections of income and financial condition for savings and loans are summarized in table 2-2. Losses in 1981 (after tax) would be between 0.60 and 0.77 percent of average assets ($4 billion to $5 billion). Should the conditions of the optimistic forecast prevail, the industry would return to normal profitability in 1982. Otherwise, the recovery would be delayed until 1983 or later. Under the pessimistic scenario, losses would occur in each year, and over the 1981–83 period would exceed $9 billion; the industry's net worth (as a share of assets) would be cut nearly in half by the end

3. Total sales of tax-exempt certificates are assumed to be approximately $81 billion at savings and loan associations and $18 billion at mutual savings banks. The major interest rate and deposit growth assumptions are as follows, given as averages over the 1981–83 period (optimistic, consensus, and pessimistic forecasts, respectively, in percentages): new mortgage contract rate for savings and loan associations (13.60, 13.98, 14.09); new mortgage contract rate for mutual savings banks (13.70, 14.08, 14.19); six-month Treasury bill discount rate (11.70, 12.71, 13.60); annual growth in retail deposits at savings and loan associations (11.03, 9.83, 7.59); annual growth in retail deposits at mutual savings banks (7.35, 6.19, 4.02).

Table 2-2. *Forecast of Income and Financial Condition, FSLIC-Insured Savings and Loan Associations*

Indicator	Interest rate forecast		
	Optimistic	Consensus	Pessimistic
Net income as share of average assets (percent)			
1980[a]	0.13	0.13	0.13
1981	−0.60	−0.69	−0.77
1982	1.04	0.21	−0.53
1983	1.09	0.58	−0.15
Industry assets, end of year (billions of dollars)			
1980[a]	609.8	609.8	609.8
1981	652.4	651.9	651.4
1982	712.8	706.8	701.3
1983	782.5	773.9	761.9
Net worth as share of assets, end of year (percent)			
1980[a]	5.32	5.32	5.32
1981	4.42	4.34	4.26
1982	5.03	4.21	3.45
1983	5.63	4.40	3.03
Associations viable only with merger, not requiring assistance			
Number of institutions	412	433	451
Percent of institutions	10.3	10.8	11.3
Total assets, end of year 1980 (billions of dollars)	22.1	24.5	26.1
Associations not viable by 1983, requiring assistance			
Number of institutions	197	347	625
Percent of institutions	4.9	8.7	15.6
Total assets, end of year 1980 (billions of dollars)	26.7	48.8	83.4
Amount of assistance required (billions of dollars)	2.5	4.1	6.4

Source: Author's estimates based on FHLBB, "Savings and Loan Activity in July," and FHLBB, unpublished data (1981). Calculations involving assets and liabilities exclude loans in process.
   a. Actual data.

of 1983. As a result of this decline in net worth and asset values, between 15 and 27 percent of the federally insured firms in the industry (609 to 1,076 associations) would find themselves in an untenable position: without drastic cost cutting, good fortune, or a cash infusion from the government, they would be unable to return to break-even operations. Ultimately, they would fail.

The solution for most of the problem institutions can be found through merger with healthier firms. Such combinations can reduce operating costs through scale economies and undertake large profitable investments that would be foreclosed to smaller associations. More than 400 of the nonviable savings and loans require only a reduction in operating costs to a level near the industry average in order to survive in the long run. These firms are attractive as merger partners and so will require little inducement by the regulatory agencies.

The remaining problem firms cannot so easily help themselves. Many will no doubt find merger partners on their own, where the synergies of a particular situation are demonstrably sufficient to offset the acquired firm's poor prospects. But there will remain a number of savings and loan associations—up to 625 firms with combined assets of $83.4 billion—that will require FSLIC assistance in merger or liquidation. The net cost to the agency for this rescue could reach $6.4 billion.

The number of firms requiring assistance may well be smaller than indicated in table 2-2, as some of these will recover or merge on their own, while no healthy firms are likely to deteriorate. On the other hand, the estimates of assistance required may be conservative. Troubled firms that begin to decline further will find the process accelerating. The volume of tax-exempt certificates they issue may be lower than the amounts assumed here. And if the FSLIC is forced to liquidate associations rather than assist them in mergers, the costs could increase by $1 billion or more.

Quite apart from these mergers of necessity, many associations will combine voluntarily for marketing or efficiency reasons; the number of firms has been contracting, and the average size growing, in good times and bad since 1960. And, again as in the past, a few associations will near bankruptcy and require FSLIC assistance because of mismanagement, fraud, or other reasons unrelated to the general financial condition of the industry.

The timing of these structural adjustments is less certain than their eventual realization.[4] It was shown earlier that savings and loan associations can generally expect a cash flow sufficient to meet their obligations to employees, depositors, and creditors. Under those conditions, an institution can continue to operate for many years with operating losses and even a negative net worth. The rate of mergers and liquidations may be relatively low well into 1982 as regulators continue to evaluate the condition of associations and await the results of policy actions and changes in interest rates. The risks in this approach are that the eventual costs may be higher if

4. During the first six months of 1981, there were seventy-four mergers and one liquidation among the 4,002 FSLIC-insured associations in existence at the end of 1980. Federal Home Loan Bank Board, "Savings and Loan Activity in July," August 28, 1981, table 3. Approximately fifty of the firms acquired would not have been viable on their own, and seven of those were merged with financial assistance from the FSLIC.

the situation does not improve, and more reorganizations may have to take place at the same time. Both these results would strain the financial and administrative resources of the regulatory agencies.

Avoiding a consolidation of the industry, preserving intact all of the troubled firms, would entail costs greater than the $2.5 billion to $6.4 billion needed for assisted mergers. To restore the firms' net worth would require capital infusions or operating subsidies totaling $5.0 billion to $11.5 billion, depending on the path of interest rates. These amounts clearly exceed the capabilities of the FSLIC. A choice to support the savings and loan industry in this manner would therefore require major new spending initiatives.

The Causes of Distress

Taking the consensus interest rate projections in table 2-2 as a basis, the characteristics leading to financial distress may be analyzed. Of course, all of the following results would be less severe under the optimistic forecast and more adverse under the pessimistic scenario.

As a group, the 780 troubled institutions, with average assets of $94 million, are much smaller than the average savings and loan association, with assets of $152 million.[5] There is a dichotomy within this group, however, between those not requiring agency assistance—the 433 voluntary merger candidates with average assets of $57 million—and the rest—the 347 critical cases that will probably require aid, with average assets of $141 million. Size could therefore explain the problems only of that subgroup that is viable under the assumption of voluntary merger.

Small institutions are not able to take advantage of all of the opportunities available to larger firms—financing large-scale real estate projects, raising funds through the sale of jumbo certificates, and diversifying loans and deposits efficiently over a wide geographic area, for example. Small institutions also tend to have higher operating costs. Several regressions were run on the data used for this study to estimate the effect of asset size on operating expenses. As seen in equations 1 and 2 in the Appendix, the average savings and loan with assets equal to those among the voluntary merger candidates ($57 million) would be expected to have operating expenses as a ratio to assets no more than 22 percent higher than an institution drawn from the population at large ($152 million in assets). Yet the voluntary merger candidates have operating expenses on average 64 per-

---

5. Loans in process are excluded from all calculations.

cent greater. The critical cases, with assets more near the average, have operating costs no higher than would be expected. So while small institutions are at a disadvantage, size does not fully explain the high operating costs of the group under consideration here. Other contributing causes are management decisions to pay high salaries to employees, officers, and directors; to build and maintain numerous large, lavish offices; and to provide a high level of service to customers. In an econometric examination of these high operating costs, both the size of the institution and this collection of other factors were found to be determinants of future operating losses (see equations 3 and 4 in the Appendix).

Many of the factors contributing to high operating costs are potentially reversible. These is substantial scope for cost reductions among the voluntary merger candidates. Cost cutting will not save the critical cases from the need for assistance, however.

Another factor reducing the prospect of viability is the below-average rate of return on assets earned by some institutions. While nearly all savings and loans are earning less than a market rate of return, the yield for some is well below the depressed level of the average. This can result from two principal factors: low yield and low turnover.

In some cases, assets were invested in investments paying less than a market return or carrying more than the market risk at the time of investment. Some of these were merely imprudent decisions. But the major reason funds went into below-market assets was regulation. In New York and elsewhere, usury laws limited the rates that could be charged on residential mortgages. So while the savings and loan industry generally is suffering from the low average return on mortgages made in the late 1960s and early 1970s, associations in some states are receiving an even lower return on mortgages of that vintage.

When there is a slow turnover of low-rate mortgages, they constitute a larger share of assets and thereby reduce the average return of the asset portfolio. Average yields can also fail to rise with increases in market rates if there are few new mortgages being issued. Mortgage-lending activity usually parallels deposit growth, as institutions are reluctant to borrow funds for lending. Savings and loan associations in areas with stable or declining populations have lower average yields than those in areas that are growing rapidly. The critical cases had virtually no deposit growth in the last six months of 1980, while the voluntary merger candidates grew 28 percent faster than the national average.

Several years of slow loan turnover, depressed earnings, and high operating costs weakens the capital position of a thrift institution. Inadequate capitalization can also result independently from management errors or from the inability to sell new stock (in the case of a stock association). Whatever the cause, low net worth can impair the ability of an association to weather a period of losses. While industry net worth averaged 5.32 percent of assets at the end of 1980, that of the voluntary merger candidates was 5.18 percent and those identified as being in serious trouble (the critical cases) averaged only 3.29 percent. Such weak starting net worth was found to be associated with long-run operating losses (see equation 5 in the Appendix).

One potential cause of high costs and low profitability—a high average rate paid on deposits and borrowed funds—was found to be a factor differentiating between firms requiring agency assistance and those that would be viable following an unassisted merger. In general, deposit rate ceilings have precluded overt rate competition for retail accounts (those under $100,000), which represent the majority of liabilities, and other instruments carry rates that are market-determined and do not vary widely across institutions. It was found, however, that some associations had a higher proportion of their deposits in high-yielding instruments and a smaller share in low-rate passbook accounts. The critical cases are likely to pay interest rates on average 1.7 percent higher (11.19 percent compared with about 11 percent) than the industry average because they have 63 percent more nondeposit liabilities and 13 percent fewer passbook accounts. Sophisticated investors and aggressive marketing by competitors could conceivably have led to this situation in one region or another.

Regional Variations in Impact

The impact of these earning pressures will not be felt uniformly across the country. Certain regions will experience a disproportionate share of the voluntary and supervisory mergers or liquidations.

As was previously discussed, low yields on old mortgages as a result of usury ceilings will continue to hamper thrift institutions in New York.[6] A low rate of mortgage turnover will add to the difficulties. The New York City metropolitan area together with Long Island has about 2.4 percent of the nation's savings and loan associations, but among those are 4.6 percent of all nonviable firms. While 19 percent of savings and loans nationwide are

6. The effective yield on mortgages held by these savings and loans was 8.6 percent, compared with 9.8 percent for all savings and loans. Author's estimates.

not viable under the consensus scenario, 38 percent of the savings and loans in New York City and on Long Island in existence at the beginning of 1981 are in that category.[7]

Savings and loan associations in Chicago are also more likely than the average institution elsewhere to succumb to economic conditions over the next few years. The problem, however, is not low earnings as in New York but rather high costs and small size. For many years, thrift institutions in Illinois were prohibited from establishing branch offices. As a result, the number of associations in Chicago proliferated. Each firm had a single office and served its own part of the city. Some branch offices were created as a result of mergers, but the average institution remained small by urban standards. At the beginning of 1981, the typical savings and loan association in the Chicago metropolitan area was only 70 percent as large as the national average for associations in urban areas. Small size and an urban location usually lead to a higher ratio of expenses to assets. The Chicago associations, however, have higher operating costs than would have been expected, suggesting extensive service competition. As a result of this situation, 37 percent of Chicago savings and loans are likely to merge or be liquidated as a result of operating losses.[8]

One other area of the country appears to have a disproportionate share of the troubled institutions. Among the associations located in the urbanized areas of Texas and Louisiana, 29 percent do not appear to be viable under the consensus forecast. These are primarily small, state-chartered, stock associations. Their problems seem to derive from high operating costs and a large share of high-rate money market and jumbo certificates among their liabilities. Passbook and other low-rate accounts represent only 14 percent of liabilities, compared with the national average of 20 percent. As these higher interest costs will drop rapidly with a fall in market interest rates, the conditions of distress in Texas and Louisiana are more likely to change than those attributable to old low-yield mortgages elsewhere; thus, the outlook for these associations may be more hopeful than the forecast indicates. However, there will probably be many voluntary mergers among these associations to improve efficiency and reduce costs.

7. Among these New York institutions, three had been merged with other savings and loans or mutual savings banks by June 1981; two of these mergers involved payments by the FSLIC. Another two New York associations were merged with FSLIC assistance in September 1981.

8. There were seven mergers (three with FSLIC assistance) and one FSLIC liquidation among this group in the first half of 1981, and one additional FSLIC-assisted merger in October 1981.

Other areas of the country have one or two adverse elements offset by certain advantages. Savings and loan associations in California pay a higher average rate on their liabilities because of their heavy reliance (double the national average) on jumbo certificates and other direct market borrowing. Yet they are able to reinvest these deposits at a favorable spread with little interest rate risk through construction financing and variable-rate mortgages. California savings and loans began offering variable-rate mortgages in 1975, well before the rest of the country, and the growing population there has contributed to a more rapid rate of mortgage origination, giving firms a higher average yield on loans and more origination fee income. Mortgages returned 11.4 percent to California savings and loans at the end of 1980, versus 9.8 percent for the nation as a whole.

Summary

Pictures of the typical nonviable savings and loan emerge: one is the voluntary merger candidate, a small but rapidly growing firm with high operating costs. Its assets and liabilities bear rates of return comparable to the national average. Cost cutting through management control and the scale economies that come with merger will obviate the need for federal assistance to this group.

And there is the critical case, a medium-sized firm in a mature urban setting. It earns less on its assets and pays more for its liabilities than the national average. Its net worth, even at book value, is substantially below the average. This is the group that ultimately must rely on the FSLIC and other agencies to meet their obligations. These firms will be merged or liquidated with government assistance.

Mutual Savings Banks

Projections for mutual savings banks are in table 2-3. While the savings banks have greater losses (as a percentage of assets) than the savings and loan associations, they also return to profitability more readily. In 1981, the industry's losses (after tax) exceeded $1 billion. The savings banks will lose nearly as much of their net worth over the 1981–83 period as the savings and loans under a given set of economic conditions, but they start from a substantially higher base: their net worth averaged 6.25 percent of assets at the end of 1980, compared with the savings and loan associations' 5.32

Table 2-3. *Forecast of Income and Financial Condition, FDIC-Insured Mutual Savings Banks*

Indicator	Interest rate forecast		
	Optimistic	Consensus	Pessimistic
Net income as share of average assets (percent)			
1980[a]	−0.17	−0.17	−0.17
1981	−0.75	−0.84	−0.92
1982	1.06	0.23	−0.62
1983	1.21	0.71	−0.02
Industry assets, end of year (billions of dollars)			
1980[a]	152.6	152.6	152.6
1981	159.9	159.8	159.7
1982	171.9	170.5	169.1
1983	186.1	183.9	181.3
Net worth as share of assets, end of year (percent)			
1980[a]	6.25	6.25	6.25
1981	5.45	5.37	5.29
1982	6.09	5.26	4.39
1983	6.79	5.56	4.08
Savings banks viable only with merger, not requiring assistance			
Number of institutions	7	11	14
Percent of institutions	2.2	3.4	4.3
Total assets, end of year 1980 (billions of dollars)	0.9	2.0	2.8
Savings banks not viable by 1983, requiring assistance			
Number of institutions	7	10	14
Percent of institutions	2.2	3.1	4.3
Total assets, end of year 1980 (billions of dollars)	14.1	19.8	22.6
Amount of assistance required (billions of dollars)	1.1	1.7	2.1

Source: Author's estimates based on Federal Deposit Insurance Corporation, *1980 Annual Report*, tables 111, 120, and FDIC, unpublished data (1981).
a. Actual data.

percent. This strong capital position will assure the continued viability of nearly all mutual savings banks under even the most adverse interest rate environment.

Only about fourteen mutual savings banks will require merger assistance from the FDIC even under the pessimistic forecast. The total claims would amount to about $2.1 billion, less than the potential costs for savings and loans, and within the resource capabilities of the insurance agency. Net costs would be somewhat less under more favorable circumstances. On the other hand, a decision to avoid mergers and restore the net worth of the existing troubled firms would entail subsidies of up to $3.4 billion.

The causes of difficulty for the mutual savings banks are somewhat different from those afflicting the savings and loan associations. There is little variation in operating expenses among mutual savings banks, and most are large enough to realize any economies of scale that exist.[9] Many of the troubled savings banks are among the largest in the industry, with average assets of more than $1 billion. Those with the weakest earnings have substantial deposit outflows (even after interest credited) and somewhat lower net worth ratios. The nonviable institutions are distributed geographically roughly as is the industry as a whole, which is to say that the troubled banks are predominantly in New York and Massachusetts.

Those requiring assistance, however, are mostly very large institutions (average assets of $2 billion), heavily concentrated in the New York City area.[10] Their problems stem from the same legacy of mortgage usury ceilings and slower mortgage turnover that has left the New York savings and loan associations in a weakened condition. Savings banks in New York also face stiff competition for deposits, which raises their cost of funds. As a result, the savings bank critical cases will earn 1.5 percentage points less on their assets and pay 0.3 percentage point more for their liabilities over the 1981–83 period than the average savings bank.

One must conclude that despite widespread disintermediation and greater operating losses, the mutual savings banks as a group are fundamentally healthy and are less likely to require assistance than the savings and loan associations. Neither liquidity shortages, reviewed in a previous section, nor the possibility of insolvency assessed here are likely to materialize for any but a handful of admittedly very large mutual savings banks. Any policy response to the problems of the thrift institutions must go beyond surface appearances and take account of the differences between the conditions of these seemingly similar types of institutions.

9. The average mutual savings bank is more than twice as large as the average savings and loan, and more than three times as large as the average commercial bank. Federal Deposit Insurance Corporation, *1980 Annual Report* (FDIC, 1981), pp. 246–51; FHLBB, "Savings and Loan Activity in July."

10. Many of these assisted mergers were in progress at the end of 1981.

Chapter Three

Criteria for Transition Policy

The current plight of the thrift institutions is the result of adverse economic conditions under an inflexible regulatory structure. Some progress has been made toward establishing a less stringent set of controls that will apply equally to depository institutions and their new competitors. Trends in interest rates and deposit flows, however, have not been favorable to the thrift institutions. Government action to address the continuing problems of the thrifts and the housing industry, beyond that mandated in recent legislation, has been proposed and will likely engender much discussion. These proposals must be evaluated in the context of the new regulatory structure.

In financial markets, as elsewhere in the economy, changes in regulations have not been implemented instantaneously. For either the imposition of new controls or the relaxation of old ones, there is usually a transition period, a time following completion of legislative or administrative action during which no changes or only partial changes are made. While there is a general notion that adjustment is time-consuming, the purpose of these lags is not addressed specifically. Delay has been used to mitigate the impact of regulatory change, to gain advantage over a rival, and to mobilize political support for rescinding the change.

The Impact of Deregulation

The system of controls in place until the mid-1970s worked tolerably well in an era of interest rate and price stability. Returning to those controls in the 1980s, as some have suggested, might produce a temporary improvement in the condition of the thrift institutions, but the force of the profit motive would soon generate innovations to circumvent the controls.[1] Acknowledging that the transition would have been easier at an earlier

---

1. See Donald D. Hester, "Innovations and Monetary Control," *Brookings Papers on Economic Activity, 1:1981*, pp. 141–89.

time, when the institutions were not so seriously threatened, does not argue for reversing the process. The problems faced today are largely not the result of deregulation; they would have occurred regardless of the regulatory environment, although they could have been more easily managed with a more timely and more complete form of decontrol.

The Depository Institutions Deregulation and Monetary Control Act of 1980 was enacted at least partly in response to the difficulties of the thrift institutions. Financial institutions were given the flexibility to adapt to changing conditions in the future. Yet the immediate transitional problems of the thrifts were also recognized, even if not fully appreciated.

The deregulation act provides only very general guidance for its gradual implementation and gives substantial discretion to the regulatory bodies. There are some physical constraints on the speed of adaptation, but these are not the factors determining the pace of the transition. Instead, issues of income distribution have been paramount, with avoidance of market disruptions another important consideration.

Institutions and individuals must adapt to the new regulatory environment in two important respects: they will modify their investment rules and the composition of their financial portfolios, and they will adjust their physical and human capital in accordance with changed incentives. These two types of adjustments—financial and real—are closely related, but it will be convenient to analyze them separately.

Financial Adjustments

The case for gradual implementation of the deregulation act to permit financial adjustments runs along two lines. In the first instance, there are arguments based on differences in the speed of adjustment, the magnitude of the required changes, and the high social cost of errors; these are generally issues that can be resolved in the short run. A second set of reasons is advanced for extending the transition period over many years: to continue existing internal subsidies, paid by depositors and other individuals, which is politically easier than authorizing direct payments to thrift institutions out of government tax revenues. The short-run case has also been advanced to justify slower deregulation in the long run.

Short run. Depository institutions are permitted to use a wider variety of asset and liability instruments as a result of deregulation. The mix of consumer deposits is changing in response to the offering of NOW accounts on a nationwide basis since January 1981. There have been flows between and

Table 3-1. *Changes in Transaction and Savings Account Composition, 1980–81*

Percent of total at end of quarter indicated

Year and quarter	Demand deposits	NOW accounts		Savings accounts	
		Banks[a]	Thrifts[b]	Banks	Thrifts
1980:1	38.5	2.1	0.7	27.4	31.4
1980:2	38.8	2.3	0.7	27.2	30.9
1980:3	38.1	2.7	0.8	27.1	31.3
1980:4	39.8	3.0	0.9	26.5	29.8
1981:1	35.9	7.2	1.7	25.8	29.3
1981:2	35.9	8.2	2.0	25.3	28.6
1981:3	36.4	9.0	2.3	24.6	27.7

Source: Federal Reserve Board, *Statistical Release H.6* (April 10, 1981; July 31, 1981; October 9, 1981), table 3A, pp. 6, 7. Figures are rounded.
a. NOW and ATS accounts.
b. NOW accounts at thrift institutions, credit union share draft balances, and demand deposits at mutual savings banks.

among banks and thrift institutions, as shown in table 3-1.[2] NOW accounts continue to be a small share of deposits at all financial institutions. The asset mix is also changing. New regulations permit thrift institutions to make consumer loans, offer credit cards, and write certain business loans. An override of state usury laws on mortgage loans gives thrifts greater flexibility. The act also imposes some new restrictions, such as reserve requirements on transaction balances and a variable level of insurance reserves.

If all of these changes were to be implemented instantaneously, an institution might find that its liability mix had shifted more quickly than the composition of its assets. The cause of timing difficulties could be differences in the speed with which borrowers and lenders reacted to new opportunities or in the pattern of adjustment in interest rates. Such a timing difference might result in transitory cash flow problems that could be avoided by pacing the two types of adjustment. These problems are analytically different from those caused by mismatched maturities on assets and liabilities.

The authorization of market-rate certificates in mid-1978 led to substantial rate deregulation for short-term liabilities, while long-term liabilities and the entire asset side remained more tightly controlled. In particu-

2. Deposit shifting from savings to transaction accounts was especially pronounced at commercial banks, where the initial interest rate ceiling for NOW accounts was set equal to the ceiling for passbook savings accounts at 5.25 percent.

lar, federal savings and loan associations were not permitted to offer a truly flexible variable-rate mortgage until 1981. Proper concern for transition problems would have argued for deregulation of long-term liabilities and the asset side well before lifting rate ceilings on short-term deposits, because the return on the mortgage portfolio adjusts more slowly.

Many of the provisions of the deregulation legislation imply potentially large adjustments. For example, thrift institutions and commercial banks that are not members of the Federal Reserve System must now maintain reserves against transaction balances for the first time. In 1981, required reserves in general were set at 3 percent of transaction balances up to $25 million plus 12 percent of such balances in excess of $25 million, and at 3 percent of nonpersonal time deposits with maturities of less than four years.[3] However, the reserve requirements, although applicable uniformly to all types of depository institutions, are being implemented on a phased schedule—eight years for thrift institutions and nonmember commercial banks and four years for large member banks.

For most of 1981, therefore, nonmember institutions' reserve requirements were only three-eighths of 1 percent on the first $25 million in NOW account balances and on all nonpersonal time deposits under four years, and 1.5 percent on NOW balances over $25 million. Cash on hand would normally be sufficient to meet these requirements, which avoids any need to place a deposit with the Federal Reserve. Thus for the thrift institutions and nonmember commercial banks, required reserves will have little substantive impact for several years, which implies that the eight-year transition period is too long. Had the full reserves been mandated immediately, however, these institutions might have been faced with a major shift in their assets.

Conversely, large member banks have been relieved of a portion of their reserve requirements. A four-year transition was provided for these reductions, not for the benefit of the banks, but to prevent a sharp increase in the money supply that would require a consequent adjustment to monetary policy.

Another reason for a transition period was to mitigate the repercussions of any unforeseen dislocations that came about from decontrol. It is important to maintain public confidence in the financial system and in the validity of the regulatory reforms. This is the problem referred to in other

3. *Federal Reserve Bulletin*, vol. 67 (July 1981), table 1.15, p. A8. Nonpersonal accounts are those held by a depositor who is not a natural person, such as a corporation.

contexts as "transitional chaos," "destructive competition," or "cutthroat pricing."[4] While there may be no more reason to anticipate such untoward results in the financial services industry than in airlines, telephone companies, or elsewhere, there are other considerations. In this case, the federal government is contractually liable, through deposit insurance and loan guarantees, for some of the losses that might be incurred and thus retains a fiduciary responsibility not present (at least to the same degree) in other sectors. Another major difference concerns the nature of the uncertainty. Elsewhere, the effect of regulatory reform has been concentrated on output prices and quantities: the railroads knew what their costs would be, even if they could not predict freight rates. But the financial institutions are facing uncertainty about both outputs and inputs. Their costs, particularly interest rates, and the availability of funds may vary widely and not necessarily in a manner consistent with output prices and quantities. And third, externalities may be more prevalent in the operation of financial institutions. The failure of a major firm can affect confidence in the entire system, an unlikely phenomenon in the transportation and public utility sector.

There is little experience with unregulated financial operations as a basis for judging the likelihood of short-run transition problems. Some evidence on deposit rate deregulation may be gleaned from the 1973 "wild card" experiment. For about four months, the regulatory agencies permitted depository institutions to offer a small certificate of deposit not subject to an interest rate ceiling. The maturity had to be at least four years and the minimum denomination of the certificate $1,000. This account proved to be popular with depositors, and savings and loan associations sold approximately $7 billion of the certificates.[5] Regulators at the time felt that the rates paid were excessive and would lead to financial instability. Ceilings were therefore reimposed. Subsequent analysis, however, has shown that rates paid on these instruments were comparable to those paid on government debt of the same maturity, as shown in table 3-2.[6] Hence there seems

4. See, for example, Andrew S. Carron, *Transition to a Free Market: Deregulation of the Air Cargo Industry* (Brookings Institution, 1981), p. 36.

5. At the time, their time deposits of all types totaled $108.3 billion. The volume of wild card certificates is the author's estimate based on Richard C. Pickering, "What Happened When the Rates Went Up? Changes in the Structure of S&L Deposits from March to September 1973," *Federal Home Loan Bank Board Journal*, vol. 7 (June 1974), pp. 21–25.

6. See Edward J. Kane, "Getting Along Without Regulation Q: Testing the Standard View of Deposit Rate Competition During the 'Wild-Card Experience,'" *Journal of Finance*, vol. 33 (June 1978), pp. 921–32.

Table 3-2. *Interest Rates Offered on Wild Card Accounts and Alternative Instruments, 1973*

Average yield in percent

| Survey date | Wild card accounts | | | Three- to five-year government bonds |
	Commercial banks	Mutual savings banks	Savings and loan associations	
July 31, 1973	7.21	7.19	7.30	7.76
August 17, 1973	7.27	n.a.	n.a.	7.80
August 27, 1973	n.a.	7.34	7.31	7.50
September 30, 1973	n.a.	n.a.	7.39[a]	6.85
October 31, 1973	7.27[a]	n.a.	n.a.	6.80

Source: Edward C. Ettin, "Petitions for Ceiling Rate Adjustments and Strategies for Deregulation," memorandum to the Depository Institutions Deregulation Committee (March 18, 1981), p. A29.

n.a. Not available.

a. Offering rates may not represent real transactions because many institutions actively offering these claims had by these dates reached their limitation that wild card accounts not exceed 5 percent of total time and savings deposits.

little reason to fear deposit rate decontrol on the basis of destructive competition, although the problems of a higher cost of funds do remain.

Long run. The arguments for extending the adjustment period beyond a few years are different in character. In an extended transition, the speed of adjustment is no longer limited by transaction constraints. The problem is that the course of regulation and economic events has created economic rents—capital gains and losses, most of them unrealized—which are distributed across institutions and individuals in a highly uneven manner. Homeowners with low-rate mortgages have gained at the expense of depository institutions, while savers have lost to banks and thrifts as a result of rate ceilings. As these assets and liabilities are "cashed out," control of resources will change hands. Deregulation speeds this process. There are windfall gains for some, the possibility of insolvency for others. As long as the transactions remain only on paper, there will be attempts to reverse the income transfers that have taken place. Delaying the full implementation of decontrol has three effects: it increases the possibility that administrative agencies, the legislatures, or the courts will halt or reverse the process; it limits the quantity of resources changing ownership; and it postpones the effects of eventual deregulation.

The difficulties of the thrift institutions must be viewed in this light. Theirs is a problem of transition only in the sense that delaying decontrol provides a partial subsidy to offset their paper losses on assets. The ultimate cost cannot be changed, although an extended transition will affect the distribution of costs and benefits.

Real Adjustments

Just as asset and liability portfolios may require a transition period in response to changing financial conditions and regulatory reform, the institutions themselves cannot adjust instantaneously to provide the new services. There are transaction lags during which institutions change their operating procedures, but these changes do not alter the relative costs and prices of services. There are also resource adjustments in reaction to changes in the cost structure; these affect the prices and quantities of services in the market.

Transactions. Financial institutions became accustomed to operating in a static environment under regulation. For thirty years following World War II, most continued to offer an array of services whose prices and quantities were largely controlled by the government. Any innovations that did take place concerned thrift institutions only indirectly.[7] Recently, however, institutions generally have sought new financial instruments and services to cope with an increasingly difficult economic environment. The number of different types of deposit and investment accounts has jumped sharply since the 1970s. Adjustable-rate mortgages, for example, are now available in a nearly infinite variety. It takes time to complete the procedural matters necessary to engage in these new activities.

Institutions must learn the characteristics of new instruments and services, set the terms for them, train their employees, secure regulatory approval where necessary, and then market the offerings. Thrift institutions and the Federal Home Loan Banks had to set up check-clearing systems before NOW accounts could be offered. New loan application forms may have to be developed, which may require advance notification of customers and regulators under the Truth in Lending Act. For their part, the regulators may wish to act slowly to avoid precipitating instability while they gather data on the progress of change.

The need for a new financial instrument may be perceived, but its propagation may be delayed by its novelty. Investors hesitate to buy new instruments offered by only a handful of institutions. Full development of these investment vehicles requires the liquidity and stability that come with widespread acceptance and the existence of a secondary market. It may be necessary for a large money center bank, the federal government, or a major secondary market agency to commit itself before a new instrument is accepted, and this learning process can be time-consuming.

7. See Hester, "Innovations and Monetary Control."

Resource adjustments. The thrift industry under regulation was characterized by extensive external and internal subsidization. Many policies were pursued to reduce the cost and increase the availability of mortgage credit through these institutions, at the expense of other capital market investments. Controls on rates and quantities promoted wide discrepancies in price-cost margins across different services. With deregulation, such variations will be eroded by market forces.

Under the deregulation act, all financial institutions can offer interest-bearing NOW accounts as an alternative to banks' demand deposit balances. Although these do not yet carry market interest rates, they are substantially more costly to the institutions than savings accounts. At first, institutions sought to equalize costs by putting restrictions on NOW accounts—high minimum balances, for example. In the long run, as these accounts begin to earn market rates of interest, market forces will not permit small-volume account holders to subsidize those who write many checks, and the cost-causing transactions will be assessed direct fees. Customers will no longer be required to hold minimum balances and will pay directly for services they receive. Institutions could become more restrictive in granting credit before deposits are cleared. The impact of these adjustments will be to reduce check-writing volume (possibly with an increase in the less costly electronic funds transfers), lower non-interest-bearing demand balances, and raise NOW account balances.

These adjustments imply major changes in institutions' cost and price structures. Although explicit pricing is inherently more efficient than cross-subsidization, consumer acceptance may be difficult to achieve. In the past, individuals have been more sensitive to user charges (such as check-writing fees) than to the opportunity cost of their funds on deposit (such as required minimum balances). The pattern of "free" checking services may persist until some event conditions public opinion and provides a focal point for several banks to simultaneously change their pricing structures. (The credit restrictions imposed by the Federal Reserve in the spring of 1980, for example, provided the focal point for many bank credit card companies to initiate annual fees, even though the logical connection between the two events was tenuous at best.)

Thrift institutions will undergo more substantial adjustments than commercial banks. Initially, they followed the lead of the banks in structuring NOW account fees, but set their prices somewhat lower. This was necessary to overcome the historical advantage of the banks in offering checking accounts. In the long run, the thrifts will face most of the pricing decisions of the banks and some others as well. In particular, regulatory restrictions and tax provisions encouraged the development of small high-cost operations. The competitive environment developing under deregulation will not permit such institutions to continue as before.

The tendency to provide more service is potentially reversible. But there are probably scale economies in the provision of financial services, implying a persistent cost disadvantage for small institutions.[8] Now that thrifts and banks must compete more fully, all institutions will seek the lowest-cost means of operation.

A clear implication of these findings is that thrift institutions, in addition to imposing charges for services, must become more efficient. This may mean closing unproductive branch offices. More likely, overlapping branch networks will be consolidated through merger of the institutions. Regulatory authorities will be receptive to such proposals, as merger is seen as a relatively costless means of rescuing the less profitable institutions.

Finally, changes in the structure and performance of the financial services industry will induce adjustments in other sectors of the economy as well. For some, the transition will imply a major reorientation. In particular, the housing and durable goods manufacturing industries are sensitive to the cost and availability of credit in the household sector. Regulation previously served to favor this group with a steady flow of low-cost financing, although rate ceilings worked at cross-purposes to the goal of increasing the quantity of deposits. Changes in policy will increase the volatility of mortgage and consumer loan rates and remove some loan rate subsidies, but they may also improve the availability of such funds during periods of monetary restraint. Thus the level of output in the housing and durable manufacturing industries could be reduced. In the absence of new subsidies, firms will have to adjust to a lower but perhaps more constant level of production, with implications for employment, investment, and choice of technology. (For example, builders might select a smaller, more highly trained work force and a more capital-intensive method of construction.)

Conclusion

The existing regulatory framework was not designed to address the transition problems faced by the thrift institutions today. Traditional tools,

8. James E. McNulty, "Economies of Scale in the S&L Industry: New Evidence and Implications for Profitability," *Federal Home Loan Bank Board Journal*, vol. 14 (February 1981), pp. 2–8; George J. Benston, "Cost of Operations and Economies of Scale of Financial Institutions," *Journal of Money, Credit, and Banking*, vol. 4 (May 1972), pp. 312–41.

such as the deposit insurance agencies and the Federal Home Loan Bank System, were developed to handle two types of difficulties: random, diversifiable, default risks and cyclical or regional variations in cash flow and profitability. It was a closed system. The costs and benefits were internalized with respect to the industry (deposit insurance) or over the business cycle (cash advances). The new transition problems involve a once-and-for-all shift in resources. Costs and benefits are no longer internal to the system; the industry as a whole has suffered a loss.

The challenge for the regulatory agencies, Congress, and the thrift industry in addressing the transition problems within the context of deregulation will be to implement a program that minimizes the disruption of financial markets and meets the tests of fairness and efficiency. Such an approach is possible if the focus is maintained on the problem institutions. As the scope is expanded to encompass healthier thrift institutions and the housing industry, the costs escalate rapidly. Given the limited resources available, the danger is that policies will be too broad, overly diffuse, and therefore both costly and inadequate to deal with the most critical problem, that of the failing thrift institutions.

There has been a massive redistribution of income from thrift institutions to mortgagors, partly offset by a shift of resources from depositors to thrift institutions. The net magnitude of this loss for the thrifts was estimated in chapter 1 at $86.5 billion by mid-1981. While only a fraction of this cost would translate into obligations of the insurance funds, the issue of what to do about that loss encompasses the profitability of the viable firms as well as the survival of the others. There are essentially only three choices: allow the situation to continue without intervention; pay the industry a direct subsidy through appropriations, tax expenditures, or off-budget activities; or establish a system of internal subsidies for the industry by delaying rate decontrol or imposing controls on competitors. These options are not mutually exclusive, and the eventual course of action will undoubtedly incorporate more than one of these types.

Under the "do nothing" option, the ultimate losers from thrift failures ordinarily would be the owners of the firm—the shareholders—and uninsured creditors. Stock savings and loan associations represent only a small share of the thrift industry, however, and the total book value of the stock is only about $1.5 billion.[9] Uninsured deposits and loans amount to substantially more, but these are concentrated at the most creditworthy institu-

9. U.S. League of Savings Associations, *'81 Savings and Loan Sourcebook* (Chicago: USLSA, 1981), p. 38.

tions. So while shareholders and uninsured creditors should be prepared to lose their investments, the major part of the loss would fall on the remaining creditors of stock savings and loan associations and the "owners" in mutual associations and savings banks, namely, the depositors. However, with the deposit insurance agencies interposed among the competing claims of insured depositors, the loss would ultimately be borne by the FSLIC, FDIC, and state insurance agencies. In effect, then, the choice to do nothing devolves to the second choice, a direct subsidy.

There is one important difference between subsidy by design and subsidy by default. If a large volume of institutional reorganizations should impair the ability of the regulatory agencies to act swiftly, there could be a crisis of confidence in the financial system. In a mild form, depositors might draw down their balances at thrift institutions, anticipating a delay in deposit insurance payments in the event of a liquidation. Of greater concern would be public doubts about the willingness and ability of the FSLIC and FDIC to honor their obligations. This perception, if widespread, could trigger withdrawals at all types of depository institutions and a flight into currency and tangible assets. The consequence for financial markets and the conduct of monetary policy would be massive disruption. These more gloomy prospects are unlikely, given the limited extent of the problem and the resources available, yet they could come to pass and it would be dereliction not to consider the possibility.

Direct subsidies paid to thrift institutions and deposit insurance agencies, therefore, would permit more careful management of the problem. However, they would be politically undesirable in a climate of budgetary restraint, so less explicit means may be used.

Direct subsidies granted through the tax system can also be effective, but many benefit in addition to the intended recipients. For example, tax-exempt savings certificates help institutions and high-income depositors, while the costs are borne by all taxpayers. Internal subsidies charge high prices (or offer low returns) to one group of firms or individuals so that another group can pay lower prices (or receive higher returns). Deposit rate ceilings, for example, subsidize depository institutions at the expense of account holders.

Economic theory and empirical evidence suggest that hidden and internal subsidies are less efficient than outright direct subsidies because they create perverse incentives and the benefits cannot easily be targeted to the most needy recipients. Yet most of the programs adopted so far, as well as those still under review, fall into these less desirable categories. Their use does have the major virtue of political acceptability, because the costs are largely hidden while the benefits can be substantial and visible. Moreover, in addition to reducing thrift failures, they channel funds into the entire industry that then become available for mortgage loans. Policies for the thrift industry are perforce policies for the housing market as well.

The responsibility of the federal government in making policy to aid the thrift industry lies on two levels. It is legally, practically, and morally obliged to aid those thrift institutions that cannot meet depositors' claims. Second, the government must decide what its role will be in helping to finance the mortgage market. Although the government is not required to support the housing industry the way it must support the thrifts, and although the trend is away from such specialized intermediaries, statements by legislators indicate that there is still a strong presumption in favor of preferential treatment for home buyers against other capital market participants.

To meet both types of responsibilities, therefore, a policy must do the following:

—compensate institutions for at least part of the loss that has been incurred;

—maintain or improve efficiency in financial markets;

—address issues of income distribution (whether on-budget or off-budget, explicit or internal) to maintain a perception of fairness and equity in government actions;

—minimize both the net cost to the government and the impact of borrowing requirements on the financial sector to be consistent with current trends in fiscal and monetary policy;

—address concerns about the health of the mortgage market and the housing industry;

—and, throughout all, maintain confidence in the depository institutions and regulatory agencies.

Chapter Four

The Policy Alternatives

An array of tools already exists to aid the regulatory agencies and the thrift institutions themselves in addressing their problems. Some were designed for other objectives, but may be appropriate for this use as well. Others were mandated by recent legislation, at least partly in response to the early signs of distress among thrifts. Many new programs have been proposed, and an important one—the tax-exempt savings certificate—was enacted as part of tax legislation in the summer of 1981. Whatever their form, the policies are intended to help the thrift industry, its customers, and related sectors of the economy. The objectives are accomplished through direct and indirect grants. There may be side effects as well, such as redistribution of income or changes in incentives.

In this section, a variety of old and new policies will be explained, analyzed, and assessed against the criteria developed in chapter 3. For expository clarity, the policy options will be grouped into five categories: direct assistance, regulatory policy, tax law, direct lending, and secondary market activities.

Direct Assistance

A policy to make direct cash grants to thrift institutions, while potentially the most efficient and effective way to meet the problem, is not likely. The Reagan administration and the current Congress are ideologically opposed to new budget initiatives, especially financial assistance to failing industries, and they have explicitly ruled out appropriations for failing thrift institutions. Nevertheless, there are already a number of mechanisms in place to provide direct aid if necessary.

Insurance Agency Assistance

In the absence of new programs, the burden of rescuing thrift institutions would fall on the Federal Savings and Loan Insurance Corporation and the Federal Deposit Insurance Corporation. The FSLIC has broad authority to subsidize a struggling savings and loan association if that will prevent a more costly failure. This may be accomplished through cash grants, subsidized loans, or purchase of low-coupon assets at face value. The FDIC may provide such financial assistance to a mutual savings bank only when preservation of the firm is essential to the well-being of the local community. Both agencies, under certain circumstances, may pay a healthy institution to assume the liabilities of a failing firm.

At year-end 1980, the FSLIC reported total assets of $6.6 billion.[1] In addition, it may borrow up to $750 million from the U.S. Treasury and may require deposits from member associations up to 1 percent of total savings. Thus the total financial resources of the FSLIC are about $12.4 billion.[2] FDIC assets totaled $11.6 billion at the end of 1980. The FDIC has authority to borrow up to $3 billion from the Treasury, giving it total resources of $14.6 billion.[3]

Based on the estimates of industry failures presented above, both insurance agencies have sufficient funds to meet the net cost of their obligations to depositors, but only barely so under the pessimistic forecast (see tables 2-2 and 2-3). The agencies could encounter substantial liquidity problems of their own, however, in conducting mergers and liquidations of firms with aggregate assets substantially in excess of their own. Recent practice has been for the FSLIC to issue promissory notes, redeemable over a period up to ten years, to firms acquiring problem institutions. Similarly, the FDIC has assumed repayment of the acquired firm's outstanding loans.[4] As an alternative to immediate cash outlays, these methods preserve the agencies' resources, although the impact on their own balance sheets may be unfavorable. The FSLIC's problems are potentially the more acute. This agency's ability to draw on the assets of its healthy members may be of little value when so much of the industry is in trouble.

Because direct federal assistance had been ruled out, the thrift institu-

1. *Federal Home Loan Bank Board Journal: Annual Report 1980*, vol. 14 (April 1981), p. 16.

2. Author's calculation based on ibid.; U.S. League of Savings Associations, *Savings and Loan Fact Book '80* (Chicago: USLSA, 1980), p. 105; Federal Home Loan Bank Board, "Savings and Loan Activity in July," August 28, 1981, table 3.

3. The insurance funds for savings banks and commercial banks are not segregated. Federal Deposit Insurance Corporation, *1980 Annual Report* (FDIC, 1981), pp. 31, 34.

4. See Paul M. Horvitz, "Insurance Agency Assistance to Failing Banks and Thrift Institutions," paper prepared for the Subcommittee on Commerce, Consumer, and Monetary Affairs of the House Committee on Government Operations (July 16, 1981), pp. 3–4.

tions' regulators (Federal Home Loan Bank Board and FDIC) joined with the Federal Reserve Board in early 1981 in proposing legislation to address the thrift industry's problems. As part of this "regulators' bill," the FSLIC asked for an increase in its Treasury borrowing line to $3 billion,[5] but was turned down by the Reagan administration. The insurance agencies have also asked for increased flexibility in using the funds they do have to provide financial assistance to troubled thrift institutions. The administration initially opposed these statutory changes as well.[6] The Treasury Department later softened its position and the House of Representatives passed the Deposit Insurance Flexibility Act (H.R. 4603) in October 1981. This legislation grants the same financial assistance powers to the FDIC currently authorized to the FSLIC, and expands the policy alternatives available to each agency, but only for a year. Although the Senate favored these provisions, the legislation before that body (S. 1703 and S. 1720) went far beyond what the House of Representatives was willing to accept in expanded asset powers for all depository institutions. The financial assistance authority common to the legislation in both houses is important for addressing the problems of the thrift industry, as was the rejected increase in FSLIC borrowing authority. All of these tools will be necessary beyond the 1982 expiration date contemplated in the House bill.

Mortgage Warehousing

One way to improve a thrift institution's earnings is to exchange the low-yield mortgages in its asset portfolio for higher-rate instruments. Under market conditions, this transaction would involve a capital loss to the institution, so that its dollar return would remain the same even as its rate of return increased. The thrift industry has proposed that the government buy these mortgages at face value, hold them a few years, and then resell them to the original institution. No capital gains or losses are recorded in this mortgage warehousing plan, giving it an initial appeal. There is a hidden subsidy, however, which is after all the reason for making the transaction. The thrift earns a high return on the cash received, while the government realizes a below-market return on the loans in the "warehouse."

Because this plan is keyed to the cause of the thrifts' problems, low-rate

5. Statement of Richard T. Pratt, chairman, Federal Home Loan Bank Board, before the Senate Committee on Banking, Housing, and Urban Affairs (April 28, 1981), p. 5.
6. See correspondence of administration officials in *Congressional Record*, daily edition, October 27, 1981, pp. H7787–92.

mortgages, funds could be directed precisely to those institutions most burdened. It is relatively efficient in that regard. To be effective, however, the value of the interest subsidy would have to be substantial—possibly larger than the net cost of assisting the troubled firms if it had to be extended to all low-rate mortgages held by both failing firms and healthy firms. Another disadvantage is that the government would have to borrow for the purchase of the assets, and even though the borrowing would be substantially offset by the acquisition of assets, it is unlikely that the capital markets would view this debt substitution (perhaps $50 billion) with equanimity. To avoid this problem and the attendant transaction costs, the government could simply pay thrifts the value of the proposed interest subsidy. But that simplification shows mortgage warehousing clearly to be the direct grant that it is.

The GNMA Tandem Plan

One function of the Government National Mortgage Association (GNMA) is to purchase low-interest mortgage loans from thrift institutions at face value and resell them on the secondary market at their lower market value. By absorbing the loss, GNMA provides a subsidy through the thrift institution: current regulations require that the institution pass along the subsidy to the borrower. This program has never been used to assist the institution itself, and its activities have been curtailed in recent years for budget reasons. The Tandem Plan is therefore an unlikely vehicle for assisting the thrift institutions.

Regulatory Policy

It is well understood that regulation can affect the distribution of income between and among suppliers and customers. Thrift institutions have sought regulatory protection from bank competition through rate ceilings, and the depository institutions as a group argue for equality with their new rivals, such as the money market mutual funds. Thrifts have also challenged their own regulators to provide them with the new powers they feel are needed to survive the current crisis—relief from usury ceilings and limits on investment, new mortgage instruments, and more lenient regulation of net worth reserves. The regulators have added their own proposals to the list, some of which (interstate and cross-industry mergers, for example) are not viewed with favor by many thrifts. And, finally, there is the role of monetary policy, a powerful but unwieldy tool.

Deposit Rate Ceilings

Regulations limiting the rates of interest that may be paid on time and savings accounts were one of the earliest policies for helping thrift institutions. Since their application to savings and loan associations and mutual savings banks on a temporary basis in 1966, they have been repeatedly reenacted by Congress. In recent years, some of these ceilings have been raised slightly, and new classes of accounts have been authorized with ceilings that vary with market rates of interest. And while the thrift industry has successfully pressured Congress into maintaining the "housing differential"—higher ceilings for thrifts than for banks—on existing accounts, this spread has been reduced and even eliminated on most new types of accounts. The differential now applies to less than half of all deposits.

The effect of binding deposit ceilings is to reduce both the quantity of deposits (through disintermediation) and the cost of maintaining deposits. In assessing the net benefit of ceilings, it is necessary to determine which effect is the larger and what the trade-off is for the institution between liquidity and earnings.

The thrift industry is of two minds on the subject of increasing rate ceilings. Some institutions with stable account bases and large sums in passbook accounts argue against raising the ceilings. They feel that the "hot money"—deposits that move from one institution to another in search of the highest return—has long since fled low-rate accounts, and that raising these rates would not affect the flow of deposits, yet the higher interest expense would impose a large loss. Of course, it is not so much a loss as an income transfer between depositors and institutions. Other thrifts, more concerned with disintermediation, want to offer competitive rates to interest-sensitive depositors. But all are agreed on the desirability of maintaining ceilings at some level and especially of keeping the differential. (Naturally, commercial bankers are strongly opposed to the differential and would like to see all rate restrictions removed.)

Decontrol of deposit rates. The issue of rate ceilings and the differential arises in the current context of policies to assist thrift institutions. Under the 1980 deregulation act, the Depository Institutions Deregulation Committee has the authority to set rates during the transition to total decontrol.

But Congress gave the DIDC little guidance, and even the basic thrust of the legislation is subject to differing interpretations: "Savings and loan associations viewed this new legislation as a six-year extension of Regulation Q and the housing differential. . . . On the other hand, commercial banks saw it as attaining their long sought goal to end the housing differential."[7] The DIDC has attempted substantive deregulation of rates in three instances; it was challenged by thrift industry lawsuits twice, and rescinded the third on its own initiative.

In the spring of 1980, short-term interest rates were falling rapidly. Treasury bill rates led the downward slide, pulling with them the rates on money market certificates at banks and thrifts. On May 28, without advance notice and following two closed meetings, the DIDC adjusted the certificate ceiling upward, narrowed the range of interest rates over which the differential applied, and decreed that the ceiling would not be reduced below 7.75 percent even if Treasury bill rates continued to decline. The committee also permitted banks to roll over maturing money market certificates at the higher thrift rate and raised ceilings on the small savers certificate. These actions were taken to forestall disintermediation, as rates on money market mutual funds remained above the ceilings called for under the old certificate formulas.

The U.S. League of Savings Associations (the savings and loan trade group) filed suit against the DIDC,[8] complaining that these actions would raise thrifts' cost of funds and divert funds from thrifts to banks. They argued that the housing industry would be further damaged. The league stated that these actions violated the law because deposit ceilings would be above market rates and because the minimum ceilings did not provide for a differential.

The problem was the deregulation act itself, which did not unambiguously require the removal of any ceilings or explicitly authorize elimination of the differential during the six-year transition period. Congress had been unable to reach agreement on whether and how to eliminate ceilings and the differential. Consider the following two paragraphs from the deregulation act:

7. Statement of Edwin B. Brooks, Jr., president, U.S. League of Savings Associations, in *Depository Institutions Deregulation Committee*, Hearings before the Senate Committee on Banking, Housing, and Urban Affairs, 96 Cong. 2 sess. (Government Printing Office, 1980), p. 63.

8. *U.S. League of Savings Associations* v. *Depository Institutions Deregulation Committee*, et al., Civil Action 80-1486, United States District Court for the District of Columbia (1980).

    (a) The Deregulation Committee shall, by regulation, . . . provide for the orderly phase-out and the ultimate elimination of the limitations on the maximum rates of interest and dividends which may be paid on deposits and accounts as rapidly as economic conditions warrant. The phase-out of such limitations may be achieved by the Deregulation Committee by the gradual increase in such limitations applicable to all existing categories of accounts, *the complete elimination of the limitations applicable to particular categories of accounts*, the creation of new categories of accounts not subject to limitations or with limitations set at current market rates, any combination of the above methods, or any other method.

    (b) The Deregulation Committee shall work toward providing all depositors with a market rate of return on their savings with due regard for the safety and soundness of depository institutions. . . . The Deregulation Committee shall increase all limitations on the maximum rates of interest and dividends which may be paid on deposits and accounts to market rates as soon as feasible, except that *the Deregulation Committee shall not increase such limitations above market rates.*[9]

Ceilings and the differential are linked. While the differential might be eliminated with a continuation of ceilings, as was done for a wide range of interest rates on the money market certificate, a ceiling cannot be removed without eliminating the differential as well.

The suit over the May 28, 1980, actions of the DIDC was decided on July 2, 1981. The court found that the DIDC had acted legally to change the rate ceilings, but that the lack of advance notice was unwarranted. The rules were not rescinded, but the DIDC was required to review the earlier decisions and follow the rules of administrative procedure.

In its second major effort to deregulate, on June 25, 1981, the DIDC adopted a plan to deregulate interest rates on time deposits. The rules called for removal of the ceiling on deposits with original maturity of four years or more, beginning August 1, 1981. Each year thereafter, the minimum maturity for deposits without any rate ceiling would be reduced by one year until, on August 1, 1985, all interest rate ceilings on all categories of time deposits would be eliminated. On the same schedule, certificates with shorter maturities than those completely decontrolled would have their ceilings indexed to the comparable Treasury issue; for these deposits, a differential of one-quarter of 1 percent in favor of thrifts would be maintained for the first two years. The U.S. League of Savings Associations challenged in court the elimination of ceilings on four-year certificates.[10] Shortly before they were to be lifted, the court enjoined the action.

9. 94 Stat. 143, sec. 204 (emphasis added).
10. *United States League of Savings Associations* v. *Depository Institutions Deregula-*

At its next meeting, on September 22, 1981, the DIDC made its third try. By a narrow margin the committee voted to raise passbook ceilings by one-half of 1 percent—to 6.00 percent for thrifts and 5.75 percent for banks—as of November 1 of that year. But a few weeks before that change was to take effect, the committee reversed itself and postponed the increase. So despite the promise of the deregulation act, the prospects for elimination of deposit ceilings remain uncertain.

The case for rate ceilings. The vigor with which the thrift industry has argued for the retention of ceilings may seem excessive. After all, virtually all new money is going into accounts offering "money market" rates. Their concern is valid, however, as ceilings continue to hold rates below the market level even on some new accounts. The true market rate for equivalent instruments is higher than the ceiling rate at depository institutions for money market certificates. The same was true until late in 1981 for small savers certificates as well. Although the difference is not large in comparison with the gap for passbook accounts, the quantity of these certificates outstanding makes the total dollar value important. Moreover, certificates do not entail the same servicing costs per dollar as the smaller accounts.

Current regulations set the ceiling yield for money market certificates at one-quarter of 1 percent over the discount rate on six-month Treasury bills.[11] The rate changes each week following the Treasury auction.[12] What is little understood, however, is that the effective investment yield on Treasury bills can be substantially more than the discount rate.[13] Even with the addition of one-quarter of 1 percent to the money market certificate rate, the underlying Treasury bill usually has the higher yield when interest rates exceed 10 percent. Moreover, from the investor's point of view, the Treasury security is to be preferred for another reason: government issues are exempt from state and local income taxes, which can cost as much as 1 percentage point on a certificate. While commercial banks and many thrift institutions could as easily sell their customers the higher-yielding Treasury bill, few go out of their way to advertise the fact.

---

tion Committee, et al., Civil Action 81-1666, United States District Court for the District of Columbia (1981).

11. This formula applies when the Treasury bill rate exceeds 9 percent.

12. Beginning November 1, 1981, the ceiling rate on these certificates was set at one-quarter of 1 percent over the four-week average of bill rates when that formula produced a higher rate than using only the most recent weekly auction results.

13. The annualized investment yield (Y) on a six-month (182-day) Treasury bill is a function of the discount rate (D) as follows:

$$Y = [\ 360\ /\ (360 - 182\ D)\ ]^{365/182} - 1$$

The situation is somewhat different for the thirty-month small savers certificate. The ceiling rate on this instrument is now pegged to a true investment yield, but for the first few months following its introduction one-half of 1 percent was subtracted. Then the ceiling was lifted to the equivalent Treasury yield, but there remained a "cap" on the ceiling at 12 percent. On August 1, 1981, this cap was removed and institutions may now pay a true market rate on deposits of thirty months or longer. These certificates still represent an advantage to the depository institution, as the penalty for early withdrawal makes them a stable source of funds. However, the interest rates may be compounded on a daily or continuous basis, raising the effective cost of these funds above comparable Treasury issues and reducing their attractiveness to institutions. Nevertheless, the cost remains below that on purchased money—jumbo certificates and borrowing.

The subsidy element in rate regulation continues to be substantial. As a rough approximation, it may be assumed that the availability of high-rate certificates for interest-sensitive depositors virtually eliminates any further disintermediation effect. It was estimated in chapter 1 that the remaining ceilings on passbook and other low-rate accounts have a present discounted value of $24.7 billion to the thrift institutions. This is the amount of the transfer to be paid by depositors over the next few years.

Estimating the impact of the rate differential is somewhat more difficult. A rigorous analysis of this policy requires observations on accounts that are similar but for the differential. With the exception of the money market certificate, however, all accounts have either had a differential throughout their existence (thanks to Public Law 94-200 and its predecessors) or have never had a differential. The experience with the money market certificate was therefore used to estimate the effect of the differential on deposit flows to thrift institutions. The quantitative effect, however, may not be as large on other, less rate-sensitive accounts.

Regression analysis indicates that reestablishing the differential on money market certificates at all levels of interest rates could significantly increase the thrift institutions' share of those funds (see equation 6 in the Appendix). The presence of a differential would increase the share going to thrifts by 6 percentage points (an 11 percent increase in funds), and decrease the share for commercial banks by the same number of points (about a 13 percent reduction for banks).[14] These values represent a substantial

14. Others have estimated the shift at approximately 10 percentage points, based on the share of money market certificates at each type of depository institution before and after the elimination of the differential. See staff memorandum to the Depository Institutions Deregu-

volume of certificates, implying a shift of about $28 billion. If there had been an interest differential on money market certificates in 1981, thrift losses would have been cut about 10 percent. Thrift industry earnings could increase by as much as $0.3 billion per year for the duration of rate ceilings if the differential were reimposed on money market certificates by lowering the ceiling for commercial banks. Bank earnings on money market certificates would increase by $0.2 billion as a result of lower interest costs, even after losing $28 billion in profitable accounts.[15] The $0.5 billion gain to institutions represents a transfer being paid by certificate holders earning lower returns at banks.

The model used in chapter 2 indicates that the net operating loss of thrift institutions would have been twice as large in 1981 had it not been for deposit rate ceilings, and if passbook rates were to increase to market level in 1982, thrift industry losses would grow by $4 billion that year and by $3 billion in 1983. Decisions on deposit rates can obviously have a major impact on thrift institution earnings during the next few years.

These gains to institutions from rate controls represent a transfer from depositors. It is this sort of inequity that the deregulation act was intended to correct. Nevertheless, given the current adverse state of industry finances, there is unlikely to be much impetus for increasing rates on passbook accounts and other low-rate small-denomination deposits. Pressure to retain the differential on most accounts will also persist, although the thrift industry has apparently lost this battle on two significant instruments, the money market certificate and the new tax-exempt certificate.

On balance, continuation of the remaining rate controls probably favors thrift institutions. The structure of ceilings and differentials now discriminates effectively between those depositors who are willing and able to pursue higher rates, and those who are content to earn a lower return. Rate controls should be viewed as an effective means of transferring substantial amounts of income from depositors to institutions. This is likely to be an important tool for the DIDC to use in improving thrift earnings and minimizing costly assistance in the next few years. For example, continued controls on passbook account rates will sustain more than 100 thrift institutions that would otherwise have required $1.5 billion in assistance from the

---

lation Committee, "Proposal to Reinstate the MMC Rate Differential," June 23, 1981. This method, however, does not account for the increasing popularity of these certificates at commercial banks before the elimination of the differential.

15. In the aggregate, bank earnings would fall as those institutions were forced to replace funds lost in money market certificates with higher-cost purchased money.

FSLIC or FDIC. Philosophically, this is antithetical to the notion of deregulation, but for practical purposes there seems to be no alternative.

Restrictions on Competitive Offerings

Representatives of the thrift industry have argued that their problems derive in part from an inability to compete with new unregulated firms. They single out the money market mutual funds, which epitomize the innovative new instruments created in response to regulatory constraints and high interest rates.[16] The money funds offer high yields on relatively small investments with excellent liquidity. The truth in the thrifts' contention is that deposit ceilings continue to limit the interest rates they may pay on retail accounts, while money funds are not comparably restricted. On the other hand, depository institutions have the benefit of FSLIC or FDIC insurance. Yet investors have apparently been persuaded that the uninsured mutual funds are safe. Since 1978, these funds have grown at an annual rate of 170 percent.[17]

Three remedies have been proposed: applying deposit rate ceilings to money market mutual funds, treating the funds as transaction accounts subject to reserve requirements, or lifting rate ceilings at depository institutions. The question is whether any of these measures is justifiable, substantive, and effective.

A case might be made that the government has an obligation to assure the viability of the thrift institutions, a duty deriving from the legacy of regulatory and tax provisions that forced them into holding long-term fixed-rate mortgages.[18] Some might feel that the government made an implicit contract to assist lenders in residential real estate. Under that premise, the effectiveness of reducing the allowable interest rate on money funds can be evaluated in terms of how effectively it would help the thrift institutions.

Interest rate ceilings. A rate ceiling on money market mutual funds would certainly make them less attractive to investors. It is less clear that the withdrawals would eventually find their way into the thrifts. Approximately 53 percent of money fund assets reside in broker/dealer accounts; many of these are the proceeds of a recent security sale invested for a short

16. See Donald D. Hester, "Innovations and Monetary Control," *Brookings Papers on Economic Activity, 1:1981*, pp. 141–89.
17. Federal Reserve Board, *Statistical Release H.6* (October 9, 1981).
18. See statement of Richard T. Pratt, pp. 9–10.

time pending another purchase. A money market certificate would not be liquid enough for those customers. Attractive alternatives to passbook savings accounts exist for such individuals, generally in the form of direct market investments. Another 19 percent are in institutional accounts, those held by bank trust departments and other fiduciaries. These investors have an obligation to seek the highest available return, and they too have access to the direct market. Only 28 percent of total money fund assets are held directly by individuals. As the average size of a noninstitutional money fund account is $14,800, it seems clear that only a small proportion of money fund assets is held by individuals whose next-best alternative would be a passbook savings account.[19] The amount of low-cost funds available to thrifts would be minimal. Thrift institutions might be more successful in attracting new deposits into money market and small savers certificates, but this should be seen more as an aid to liquidity than as an improvement in earnings.

The effect of money market mutual funds on deposit flows to thrift institutions was estimated in a regression (see equation 7 in the Appendix). The results show that higher rates available from the money funds have had a small negative impact on the flow of deposits to thrift institutions. For each percentage point that the money fund yield exceeds the yield on money market certificates at thrifts—historically, the gap has averaged half a point—the thrift institutions lose approximately 1.5 percent of the gross money invested in a month (new money invested plus maturing time deposits rolled over). This translates to between $1 billion and $2 billion per month. It would appear that the higher rates available on money market mutual funds have played at most a minor role in causing the problems of the thrift institutions.[20]

For practical and legal reasons, it might be difficult to limit returns on money market mutual funds even if it were deemed desirable. Partly it is an issue of definition. Money funds are "regulated investment companies" under the Internal Revenue Code, just as are the traditional stock and bond mutual funds. There is no legal distinction between the two types of funds: the principal differentiating factor is the average maturity of their assets. A

19. Figures on money funds from Investment Company Institute, unpublished data (Washington, D.C.: ICI, 1981).

20. It is possible that the money funds did not begin to have an effect until 1980, when the general public became aware of their existence. Equation 7 was reestimated for the June 1978–December 1979 period. Projections based on this truncated period indicate a slightly greater impact from the money funds by 1981, but the two equations were not significantly different based on the Chow test.

restriction on money funds would necessarily affect stock and bond funds as well, an undesirable and unintended result. Furthermore, if any mutual fund were to earn substantially more than the amount it was permitted to pay out, it would lose its tax exemption. A simple extension of interest rate ceilings to the money funds would virtually destroy the mutual fund industry.

Reserve requirements. A somewhat stronger justification can be advanced for a weaker measure to limit returns on money market mutual funds. It is said that investors use their money fund accounts as a substitute for checking or NOW accounts at depository institutions. Banks and thrifts must hold reserves against transaction accounts, so if money fund accounts are de facto transaction balances, there is an inequity.[21] But the overall evidence shows major differences between demand deposits and NOW accounts on one hand and savings accounts and money funds on the other. Moreover, requiring money funds to hold reserves would have little effect on the yields and on the availability of funds to thrifts, and even these minor impacts could be easily evaded by the money funds.

The Depository Institutions Deregulation and Monetary Control Act (section 103) requires depository institutions to maintain reserves against transaction accounts, defined as follows:

> (C) The term "transaction account" means a deposit or account on which the depositor or account holder is permitted to make withdrawals by negotiable or transferable instrument, payment orders of withdrawal, telephone transfers, or other similar items for the purpose of making payments or transfers to third persons or others. Such term includes demand deposits, negotiable order of withdrawal accounts, savings deposits subject to automatic transfers, and share draft accounts. . . .
>
> (E) In order to prevent evasions of the reserve requirements imposed by this subsection, . . . the Board of Governors of the Federal Reserve System is authorized to determine, by regulation or order, that an account or deposit is a transaction account if such account or deposit may be used to provide funds directly or indirectly for the purpose of making payments or transfers to third persons or others.[22]

The nature of money market mutual fund accounts that permits redemptions by check would clearly put them within the purview of this section, except that they are not depository institutions. At the least, it would ap-

21. See statement of Paul Volcker, chairman, Board of Governors of the Federal Reserve System, before the Subcommittee on Domestic Monetary Policy of the House Committee on Banking, Finance and Urban Affairs, June 25, 1981.
22. 94 Stat. 133.

pear that provisions of law other than this act would have to be invoked to apply reserve requirements to money funds.

In practical terms, however, the check-writing feature of money funds is of little importance. Generally, checks drawn on money fund accounts must be for $500 or more. Often the check is used merely as a means of transferring funds between two accounts owned by the same investor, a transaction not covered by the legislation on reserves. Only two checks per year are written against the average money fund account.[23] While this feature is perhaps useful as a marketing tool, the money fund account is not used by most investors as a substitute for a checking account. Otherwise the data would show that money market fund accounts turn over more rapidly than they do. Total demand deposit turnover at commercial banks, reflecting a high percentage of commercial accounts, was 201.6 during 1980 and 260.9 annual rate for the first five months of 1981. Automatic transfer and NOW accounts at commercial banks turned over at a 9.7 rate in 1980 and a 13.5 rate in 1981, while savings accounts averaged 3.4 times in 1980 and 3.3 times in 1981.[24] Despite rapid growth in money market funds, however, the turnover rate has remained very low: 3.0 times in 1980 and 3.1 times at an annual rate for the first seven months of 1981.[25] These figures suggest that money funds could easily rescind or restrict the check-writing feature if they felt it necessary to avoid reserve requirements.

Initially, however, the impact of reserves would be slight. As described earlier, the new reserve requirements are being imposed in phases. A 17.50 percent money fund yield would be reduced to 17.42 percent in the first year, and to 17.16 percent in the second year by the holding of non-interest-bearing reserves in excess of cash on hand.[26] The regression results cited earlier suggest that this diminution of yields would not materially help the thrift institutions.

It has also been noted by representatives of the investment company industry that money market mutual funds hold a portion of their assets in certificates of deposit at U.S. banks, and that these deposits are subject to reserve requirements. To impose reserves on that portion of assets, they

23. Estimate provided by Investment Company Institute.
24. Demand deposit turnover is defined as debits divided by average balance. *Federal Reserve Bulletin*, vol. 96 (July 1981), p. A12.
25. Money fund turnover is gross redemptions (all types—check, wire, mail) divided by average assets. Investment Company Institute, unpublished data (1981).
26. The effect at lower interest rate levels would be even smaller. Author's estimates based on Federal Reserve Board, *Statistical Release H.6*, selected issues; and *Federal Reserve Bulletin*, vol. 96 (July 1981), p. A48.

reason, would be inappropriate. While true, this counterclaim is of minor importance. Less than 30 percent of money fund assets is in reservable instruments, and the reserve percentage applicable is only one-quarter the level on transaction accounts.[27]

Summary. Imposing restrictions on money market mutual funds would seem to offer little amelioration of the thrift institutions' predicament. Moreover, even by the admission of their advocates, controls would run contrary to the policy of deregulation:

> In the absence of an appropriate competitive ability on the part of regulated financial institutions, we believe it would be appropriate for Congress, on a strictly interim basis, to enact legislation that would ensure a greater degree of competitive equality between MMFs and depositories than now exists. . . . As a free-market economist, I am not happy to make this recommendation. But, there are periods when controls are necessary, and this is one of them.[28]

Rate ceilings and reserve requirements on money funds would be difficult to implement and would be generally ineffectual. The only way to beat the money funds is to confront their strengths.

The removal of deposit rate ceilings at banks and thrift institutions would trigger an irreversible decline in assets at money market mutual funds. Depository institutions can offer all of the advantages of money funds as well as serving a customer's other financial needs—loans, credit cards, check cashing, trust and safe deposit services, utility payments. If the eventual decontrol of rates mandated by the 1980 act comes to pass, the money funds will lose their special niche as all financial institutions begin to offer a variety of highly liquid market-rate accounts. Yet they may have a slight reprieve, as the thrift institutions continue to campaign against a lifting of rate ceilings.[29]

Expanded Asset Powers

The thrift institutions' problems derive in large part from the preponderance of a single type of investment in their asset portfolios—the long-term fixed-rate residential mortgage. Regulations and tax laws precluded insti-

27. Investment Company Institute, unpublished data (1981).
28. Statement of Richard T. Pratt, p. 9.
29. See Timothy Q. Cook and Jeremy G. Duffield, "Money Market Mutual Funds: A Reaction to Government Regulations or a Lasting Financial Innovation?" *Economic Review*, vol. 65 (Federal Reserve Bank of Richmond, July–August 1979), pp. 15–31; and Robert W. Eisenmenger, "The Experience of Canadian Thrift Institutions," in *The Future of the Thrift Industry*, Conference Series No. 24, *Proceedings of a Conference Sponsored by the Federal Reserve Bank of Boston*, October 1981 (Federal Reserve Bank of Boston, forthcoming).

tutions from doing much else. Now, removal of those restrictions has been proposed.

The expanded asset powers permitted by the Depository Institutions Deregulation and Monetary Control Act and those proposed in subsequent reform legislation are intended to foster equality among financial institutions. The new instruments have the advantages of short maturities and high (market-level) interest rates, virtues especially desirable when the yield curve is flat or inverted. Moreover, the faster turnover of these instruments will improve the cash flow of the institutions far more than their small share of total assets would suggest. For example, shifting only 20 percent of a long-term asset portfolio into short-term consumer loans would shorten turnover for the whole portfolio from once in ten years to once in four. The ability to offer a wider variety of financial services can have an additional benefit: depositors may be more willing to accept lower deposit rates in exchange for the convenience of "one-stop" banking.

Thrift institutions are moving slowly, however, to take advantage of their increased asset powers. To make major nonmortgage investments would also require changes in the tax law applicable to thrift institutions.[30] Improved earnings will come about only as old mortgages are repaid and the proceeds are directed to the new investments. And expanded asset powers are not a panacea. Thrifts will have to compete directly with more experienced banks and finance companies for this business. Consumer loans and other nontraditional investments carrying higher returns and shorter maturities will entail high transaction costs and greater default risk, and there is the threat of usury ceilings and other limitations being imposed at the state level. While a more diversified asset mix is clearly desirable, its eventual benefit will be to moderate the impact of interest rate swings rather than to increase the profitability of the thrifts.

Thrift institutions can insulate themselves from much of the interest rate risk and still invest in residential loans by using one or more of the new variable-rate mortgage instruments. Although the variety of these innovations is so great as to make generalization difficult,[31] they share a number of common features: they are long-term amortization loans, which protect borrowers from balloon payments and refinancing problems; the loan interest rate, and therefore the monthly payment and/or the loan term, varies

---

30. See statement of Richard T. Pratt, pp. 16–17.

31. For a summary of the characteristics of these alternative mortgage instruments, see Henry J. Cassidy, "Price-Level Adjusted Mortgages Versus Other Mortgage Instruments," *Federal Home Loan Bank Board Journal*, vol. 14 (January 1981), pp. 3–11.

with changes in market rates; and the initial rate on a variable loan is typically below that on a comparable fixed-rate loan, reflecting the smaller interest rate risk assumed by the lender. The implications of shifting the risk from lender to borrower are only beginning to be understood. Residential real estate prices, for example, will be affected by these new financial arrangements.

Futures market transactions are an alternative to adjustable-rate mortgages that accomplish the same diminution of interest rate risk for institutions, but relieve households of that risk as well. Savings and loan associations were authorized in 1981 to hedge, that is, take long positions in forward markets up to the amount of their exposure to interest rate swings. A disadvantage is that the price of the forward commitment may not move precisely inversely with the value of the mortgage loan portfolio.

The issue here, however, is what role variable-rate mortgages or hedging can play in assisting the recovery of thrift institutions. Unfortunately, the answer is that the new mortgage investments and futures contracts offer significant help only in the long run. Over the next few years, they are at best a minor boon for the thrifts. On the plus side, more loans will be written than if only the fixed-rate type were available or if hedging were not permitted. This will improve cash flow and asset portfolio yield and generate additional fee income as well. Both lenders and borrowers do find the new mortgages attractive. Disadvantages for the institution, however, are that cash flow is lower at first with some types of variable-rate loans, the secondary market for mortgages and the mortgage futures market are not yet well developed, and the possibility of repayment delinquency with variable-rate loans may be a threat if rates rise sharply.

Variable-rate mortgage loans and hedging, like the other departures from the thrift institutions' traditional investments, are crucial to the long-term viability of the industry and will provide some earnings improvement during the next few years. Certainly, the expansion of thrifts' asset powers even as late as 1978 would have substantially reduced the magnitude of their current difficulties. But with continued sluggishness in the housing market due to high interest rates and slowing economic growth, neither variable-rate mortgages nor futures market transactions can be viewed as a major policy tool for preventing near-term disruptions and minimizing federal assistance.

There is one change in asset powers that could have an immediate beneficial effect on thrift earnings. This is the proposal to override state laws that prohibit lending institutions from enforcing the due-on-sale clause in mortgage contracts. If this is enacted, many low-rate mortgages will be repaid because they cannot be assumed by the purchaser, and new mortgages will be written at a higher rate.

Balance Sheet Regulation

Regulatory authorities in the past have moved to reorganize ailing thrift institutions well before insolvency was reached. Savings and loans are normally required to maintain net worth in excess of 4 percent of deposits. Mutual savings banks in New York state must seek regulatory permission to pay dividends to depositors when their net worth falls below 5 percent of deposits, and other states have similar laws. One current policy to forestall intervention by the regulators has already been implemented. Simply stated, the standards have been lowered. Thrifts are permitted to continue in operation under circumstances that previously would have closed their doors.

Obviously, these shifts do nothing to alter the fundamental condition of the institutions. What does change is the timing of supervisory activity. Confronting the issue of insolvent institutions is delayed, awaiting lower interest rates or new subsidies. Assuming that future economic conditions or government assistance render weak institutions viable once again, this policy has the advantage of preserving the industry much as it is. It also permits the regulators to deal with failing institutions in a deliberate manner by postponing many closings until the resources become available. The principal disadvantage is that the ultimate costs of assistance can escalate during the period of delay as the institution suffers continuing erosion of its net worth. Ultimately, the wisdom of this policy depends on the likelihood of future events. As the prospect of substantially lower interest rates fades, and as new government assistance appears limited to the tax-exempt savings certificate, the time may be at hand for accelerating the pace of supervisory mergers and liquidations of nonviable thrift institutions.

Two variants of this net worth policy have been developed. The first, adopted by the FSLIC in September 1981, calls for the agency to issue cash and/or promissory notes to troubled mutual savings and loan associations. These contributions would be included in assets, thereby augmenting net worth. In exchange, the FSLIC would receive income capital certificates. Interest and repayment of principal to the insuror would be contingent on the institution's return to profitability. In the event of liquidation, the claims of the holder of income capital certificates (the FSLIC) would be subordinate to all other creditors.[32]

A second plan involving accounting changes was also adopted in late 1981. Accounting rules had previously required an institution to recognize gains and losses on the sale of mortgages in the year that the transactions occurred. Thus an institution that wanted to realize losses for tax purposes, or modify the maturity structure of its portfolio through asset sales, might have been inhibited from making those transactions because the resulting net worth would fall below the regulatory minimum. Such sales can increase market-value net worth even while they decrease book-value net worth. To encourage sound portfolio management, the Federal Home Loan Bank Board now allows savings and loan associations to amortize losses on mortgage sales over several years for purposes of calculating regulatory net worth. This plan represents an awareness that accounting conventions based on original costs (book value) can be misleading. It also permits a realization of tax refunds through loss carry-back provisions; the subsidy element is small, however, in that principally it is the timing and not the magnitude of the tax savings that is changed. This proposal is timely and consistent with administration policies. However, it will provide only modest benefits to those institutions most in need of assistance, whose tax credits may be exhausted and whose net worth may already be at subminimum levels. The practice also violates generally accepted accounting principles, and thus cannot be used by a stock association in public financial statements.

The Federal Home Loan Bank Board took another decision in mid-1981 to increase flexibility for savings and loan associations. It withdrew a proposed restriction on the amount of goodwill an FSLIC-insured association may include in its assets as a result of the acquisition of another association. When the assets of the acquired firm have a market value below book value, the rules permit the acquiring firm to value tangible assets (such as mortgages and consumer loans) at market value, thereby showing a market rate of return. Ordinarily the difference between book value and market value would reduce total assets and net worth. The accounting rules permit this difference instead to be attributed to goodwill acquired, an asset item.

32. A similar plan has been proposed for stock savings and loan associations. In that case, the FSLIC's claims would precede those of shareholders. For a complete description of income capital certificates, see Douglas P. Faucette and Richard K. Kniepper, "Income Capital Certificates: FSLIC Creates a Unique Savings and Loan Security," *Federal Home Loan Bank Board Journal*, vol. 14 (October 1981), pp. 10–13.

Book-value net worth is unaffected. By permitting this practice to continue, whatever its shortcomings as an aid to financial analysis, the board has facilitated voluntary mergers. Goodwill acquired in this manner has no earning capacity and thus provides little benefit to the seriously troubled firms. The virtue of the practice is that it permits economically sound mergers that might otherwise be precluded by accounting conventions.

Merger Policy

The regulators' bill and subsequent legislative proposals discussed earlier sought to establish guidelines for mergers involving problem institutions. Mergers across state lines and between banks and thrifts have traditionally been prohibited. Large commercial banks and some thrifts have expressed a strong desire to expand across state lines because of the profit opportunities and competitive advantages of large scale and of geographically extensive operations. The FSLIC already has the authority to approve interstate mergers for troubled savings and loan associations, and the Federal Reserve Board is empowered to authorize the acquisition of thrifts by commercial bank holding companies. Approval of an interstate or cross-industry merger may be likened to a license that can be offered for sale. The price of that license would be the excess of liabilities over assets for a failing thrift institution, a price that would have to be paid by the FSLIC or FDIC if the license is not sold.

Two major objections, one practical and one philosophical, have been raised to this plan. The practical obstacle is that there are not enough large banks and thrifts seeking interstate authority. Recall that up to 625 very troubled savings and loans and 14 sizable mutual savings banks (the critical cases) must be merged or liquidated. There are only about 300 depository institutions of all types with assets over $1 billion[33] (the size most likely to initiate interstate operations), and a quarter of those are thrift institutions with problems of their own. The weak thrifts are concentrated in a few locations, notably New York and Chicago, where the large money center banks have already established a presence. A few problem institutions in sun belt states might be attractive targets, but the majority located in the Northeast and Midwest would not. One way of partially overcoming this drawback, appropriating more of the value of an interstate franchise for public purposes, is to offer the privilege only as a multifirm deal: the

33. FDIC, *1980 Annual Report*, p. 234; U.S. League of Savings Associations, *Fact Book '80*, p. 53.

right to acquire one desirable thrift institution would be contingent on rescuing one or more other troubled-firms elsewhere in the country. But legislation before Congress would compel a reliance on mergers primarily between thrifts and within states, thereby limiting the use of mergers to relieve part of the financial burden on the deposit insurance agencies.

Philosophically, it is inappropriate to consider the issue of interstate branching strictly in the context of the thrift institution problem. Relaxation of branching laws would initiate a major restructuring of the financial sector that should be evaluated on its own merits, apart from whatever benefit the thrifts may derive. There has been a tradition in antitrust law and elsewhere of favoring the small locally owned enterprise. Restrictive branching laws for depository institutions are one manifestation of this. The concern is that a system with a few large centrally controlled firms would lead to monopolistic practices and inattention to local needs. It has not been demonstrated that these results are likely or even possible. Nevertheless, a policy that relies on substantial consolidation of the industry, whatever its other merits, must not exceed the bounds of an acceptable concentration of power.

The thrift problem, serious as it is, remains one of transition. Interstate banking is an irreversible change with far-reaching implications.[34] Although it may eventually be decided that interstate banking is desirable, it would be imprudent to end the long-standing prohibition without a public airing of all the issues involved.

Deposit Insurance Enhancement

Savings, certificate, and transaction accounts at most depository institutions are insured up to $100,000 by the FSLIC or FDIC. The claims of other account holders and creditors, including those holding repurchase agreements, are subordinate to those of the insured depositors. In a crisis, the liabilities not covered by insurance might be withdrawn for fear of default. If the resources of the insurance agencies were called into question, withdrawals by insured depositors could precipitate a liquidity shortage. It has been suggested, therefore, that federal insurance cover all deposits, and that protection of these deposits be made an explicit obligation of the federal government to the extent they exceed the assets of the insurance funds.

34. See Lawrence G. Goldberg, "Bank Holding Company Acquisitions, Competition, and Public Policy," in Lawrence G. Goldberg and Lawrence J. White, eds., *The Deregulation of the Banking and Securities Industries* (Lexington Books, 1979), pp. 219–42.

Alternatively, a merger of the FDIC and FSLIC insurance funds might be sufficient to allay concerns over default.

The foregoing analysis suggests that insured depositors in fact have no cause for concern. Enhancement of deposit insurance would therefore appear to be a relatively costless policy. On the other hand, it should be seen principally as a means of maintaining liquidity, with little effect on earnings.

Monetary Policy

Reducing the level of market interest rates would, of course, restore some of the value of thrift institution assets. For market value to rise to book value, long-term rates would have to remain below 12 percent during 1982 and 1983. Short-term rates of 10 percent would then restore normal operating margins. Given the current macroeconomic policy, however, this seems unlikely. The consensus appears to call for restricting the growth of the monetary aggregates to reduce inflation while pursuing an essentially neutral fiscal policy. While this mix may be successful in reducing inflation, and therefore interest rates, over the long run, relief in this form would come too late to aid the thrift institutions.

Tax Law

The tax system has long been used as an alternative to appropriations for giving preference to certain activities. Thrift institutions have enjoyed favorable tax treatment, which has permitted them to make mortgage loans at less than market rates. Another effect of the tax laws has been to encourage large additions to reserves (net worth), a legacy that is now proving fortuitous. Current policy initiatives have been focused on the individual income tax, although proposals have also been advanced to change the tax provisions applicable to thrift institutions.

Tax-exempt Savings Accounts

After the thrift industry and its regulators were rebuffed in their attempts to get either direct cash assistance or increased borrowing authority from the Reagan administration, representatives of the industry approached Congress with a proposal to subsidize thrifts through the tax system. This "All Savers Act" was drafted by the U.S. League of Savings Associations to provide for a tax-exempt savings certificate. The account was to be available only to individuals and only at depository institutions, would carry a one-year maturity, and would have a yield exempt from federal income taxes set at 70 percent of the comparable Treasury bill rate. The issuer would profit on the spread between its cost (the rate on these certificates) and the substantially higher rates available on investments in the taxable market. Purchasers in high tax brackets would benefit from a tax-free return that was higher than the after-tax return on alternative instruments. The costs of the subsidy (tax expenditure) would fall on the Treasury from revenue losses.

The legislation was proposed as a way "to promote additional savings, foster capital formation and provide badly needed cost relief to depository institutions and their beleaguered customers, most notably in housing, small business, and agriculture."[35] It was not specifically suggested that enactment of this provision would prevent thrift failures, reduce the number of forced mergers, or limit the exposure of the deposit insurance funds. The industry, however, has never publicly admitted the possibility of a substantial consolidation such as has been suggested here. Such an eventuality nevertheless is implicit in statements such as "the number of savings associations whose net worth is approaching zero is rising at an alarming rate."[36] The alacrity with which members of Congress embraced the act suggests that fears of collapse may indeed have been mixed with a general concern over the health of a number of thrift-related industries such as construction and real estate.

The plan proposed by the representatives of the thrift industry was incorporated with only minor changes in the Economic Recovery Tax Act of 1981.[37] The certificates are being offered during a fifteen-month period beginning October 1, 1981, only a few months after the originally suggested starting date. Individuals may exclude from their taxable income up to $1,000 in interest on these certificates, and married couples filing jointly may claim $2,000. All depository institutions may issue the certificates (including credit unions). Commercial banks, savings and loans, and mutual savings banks must suspend sales at the end of a calendar quarter if they have not invested a certain portion of their increased deposits in resi-

35. U.S. League of Savings Associations, "The Economic and Tax Revenue Impact of H.R. 3456 and S. 1279: The All Savers Tax Act," news release, June 10, 1981, p. i.
36. Ibid., p. 5.
37. 95 Stat. 171.

dential and agricultural loans. The investment requirements, however, are set at levels conforming to the industry's average historical experience. To minimize the revenue loss from savings incentives in the tax code, Congress suspended for two years the one deduction truly benefiting all savers—the exclusion from taxable income of a portion of any interest received during the year. And Congress dropped the term *all savers* from the bill, calling these accounts "depository institution tax-exempt savings certificates."

It is anticipated that these certificates ultimately will be purchased by a large share of the taxpayers in high brackets. Generally, a taxpayer would have to be in a bracket above 30 percent for the certificate to have an after-tax yield higher than the Treasury bill on which its rate is based. The limiting bracket could be somewhat higher where there are state income taxes. In comparison with the transferable Treasury bill, the tax-exempt certificate may be redeemed prior to maturity only by forfeiting some of the interest accrued and the tax exemption. On the other hand, the tax-exempt certificate offers a higher yield than passbook accounts, a shorter maturity than the small savers certificate, a smaller minimum denomination than the money market certificate ($500 versus $10,000), and the security of deposit insurance. The tax-exempt certificate may therefore be attractive to some individuals in low tax brackets.

The extent of "all savers" certificates. Developing a forecast of the number of such certificates likely to be sold thus requires data on several factors: the path of interest rates, the shape of the yield curve, marginal tax rates, wealth, the trade-off between return and liquidity, and the extent to which individuals will act rationally and with adequate information as to the tax consequences of their investments. The results affect not only the finances of the thrift institutions, but income distribution, the housing market, and the size of the government deficit as well.

The congressional Joint Committee on Taxation estimated that $3.3 billion in federal revenue will be forgone because of tax-exempt savings certificates.[38] This figure implies certificate sales of approximately $70 billion. Other estimates have ranged to $180 billion[39] and higher, albeit under scenarios of higher tax rates and lower interest rates. (Tax reductions make the certificates less attractive to some investors, and since the interest ex-

38. *Summary of H.R. 4242: The Economic Recovery Tax Act of 1981*, prepared by the staff of the Joint Committee on Taxation (GPO, 1981), p. 60.

39. Statement of Donald Morton, U.S. League of Savings Associations, before the Subcommittee on Savings, Pensions, and Investment Policy of the Senate Committee on Finance, May 4, 1981.

emption is limited to $1,000 per individual, the higher the interest rate the lower the principal amount of the certificate that qualifies.) Further analysis of the Joint Committee estimates indicates that depository institutions would save about $2.5 billion in interest costs (before tax): $1.1 billion at banks and $1.4 billion at thrift institutions.[40] The remaining $0.8 billion of the revenue loss would accrue as a tax saving to high-income taxpayers, generally those earning over $30,000 per year.

The Brookings Institution tax file was used to generate an independent estimate of the likely volume of tax-exempt certificate sales. It was assumed that individuals above the 30 percent bracket in 1982 would shift a substantial portion of their assets into tax-exempt certificates. The volume of certificates purchased was restricted to that which produces $1,000 per year per person in tax-exempt interest over the tax years 1981–83. The results of this computation indicate total certificate sales of $85 billion to $105 billion. Gross revenue losses of $5.1 billion over three years would accrue as a $0.7 billion tax reduction for individuals, with more than half of that going to families with annual incomes over $50,000, and a $4.4 billion increase in depository institutions' before-tax income.

If the tax-exempt certificates are successful in attracting funds away from money market mutual funds and direct market investments, they will improve the liquidity of depository institutions as well as their earnings. As much as three-fourths of the funds, however, are expected to come from other accounts at depository institutions—primarily money market certificates, which have after-tax yields, maturities, and denominations similar to the tax-exempt certificate.[41] And illiquidity was not considered a serious concern in any case.

The tax-exempt certificates will improve earnings for the thrift industry, not only during the years in which they are outstanding, but for long afterward even if all of the deposits are withdrawn upon expiration of the program. That is because the reduction in operating losses for 1981, 1982, and 1983 will preserve more of the institutions' assets, the major determinant of gross income over the long run. Using the consensus forecast of interest rates and the accounting model described earlier, the impact of these certificates on the thrift industry can be evaluated in a quantitative fashion.

An optimistic assumption was made regarding the volume of certificates

40. Author's estimates, assuming a division of certificates among institutions equivalent to the current allocation of new investments in money market and small savers certificates.
41. Early data are consistent with these predictions. See FHLBB, "Savings and Loan Activity in September," October 31, 1981, p. 1.

to be sold by thrift institutions: $81 billion by savings and loans and $18 billion by mutual savings banks. For the savings and loan associations, the assumed substantial sales of tax-exempt certificates would turn combined losses over the 1981–83 period of $1.3 billion (after tax) into a profit of about $1.4 billion—roughly a $1 billion improvement in earnings for each $30 billion in certificates. Annual net income after 1983 would be higher by 0.02 percent of assets; normal earnings are in the range of 0.70 to 0.80 percent of assets. Approximately 2 percent of the associations (seventy-two savings and loans) viable under the consensus economic scenario would not have been viable over the long run without the tax-exempt savings certificate. The model predicted a $0.4 billion after-tax profit in 1981–83 for the mutual savings banks, but indicated a loss of $0.4 billion without the certificate. The number of viable savings banks would be unaffected.

Of particular interest is the efficiency of this program in ameliorating the impact of high interest rates on the weakest institutions. It was estimated that assisted mergers and liquidations in the savings and loan industry will cost the FSLIC $4.1 billion (net); this is based on the consensus forecast, with the tax-exempt certificate. Under the same economic conditions, but without the certificate, this cost would have been $4.5 billion. (The gross amount of industry assets involved would have been increased from $48.8 billion to $54.6 billion.) The impact upon the total FSLIC liability is thus minor. What is more, it still leaves 780 savings and loan associations in an unsustainable earnings situation. As a means of averting widespread consolidation and minimizing the need for federal assistance to the thrift industry, therefore, the tax-exempt certificate is both ineffective and inefficient.

But rescuing the thrift industry was not necessarily the principal aim of the tax-exempt certificate. The program may be successful in inducing increased net savings by individuals, although its limited duration and the restriction on total interest earned will dilute this effect. As with any tax deduction, there is also an impact on the distribution of income. This plan provides the most substantial benefits to high-income taxpayers and to thrift institutions. It may permit the thrifts to increase their lending activities, to the extent that the funds in certificates remain on deposit after the expiration of the program.

Limited Partnerships

Another proposal to subsidize thrift institutions through the tax system involves the formation of limited partnerships with outside investors. A portion of an institution's low-yield mortgages would be sold on the open market at a loss, which the investors would be permitted to deduct from their own taxable income. The investors would then add cash to the proceeds of the sale of mortgages and invest in new mortgages earning market rates. Investors and institutions would share in the increased earnings. The plan gives both partners a higher present value after-tax return: the deduction for the loss on the sale of mortgages is greater when claimed in one year by individuals in the 50 percent bracket than when taken over a span of years by a savings and loan, which pays taxes at a rate of approximately 30 percent. This plan would require tax expenditures as large as the amount of the firm's negative net worth to restore viability. Moreover, targeting to the weakest institutions would be difficult since investors would prefer the stronger ones. The net cost in forgone tax revenues might be reduced if it is assumed that investors in a thrift partnership would otherwise have sought some other tax shelter, which would be replaced by the thrift partnership.

Proponents of the partnership plan are seeking tax and regulatory approval. Congressional action may be required. Despite the obstacles, it is probable that some benefits will eventually flow to thrifts through this device.

Tax Changes for Institutions

Thrift institutions pay little tax under current law when operating income is negative, so the opportunity to provide them with further direct assistance through the tax system is limited. They are entitled to a ten-year carry-back of net operating losses and a five-year carry-forward. As a result, thrift institutions now operating at a loss are receiving substantial refunds of tax paid in earlier years. A 1979 ruling by the Internal Revenue Service had the effect of reducing the value of loss carry-backs by 40 percent.[42] The Federal Home Loan Bank Board formally asked Congress to overturn the ruling and reestablish prior law. To do so would cost the federal government as much as $1 billion if applied to thrift institutions in 1981 and later tax years, an amount that would be reflected in a commen-

---

42. Essentially, the ruling requires institutions to recompute their entire profit and loss statements for the earlier years, thereby reducing the amount of certain deductions based on before-tax income taken in those years. Prior practice allowed the loss carry-back to be applied to final taxable income in the earlier years. The estimate of the amount of the reduction is based on the value of the before-tax deductions, and is from statement of Richard T. Pratt, p. 12.

surate improvement of the industry's income statement.[43] Although the effect of this tax change has not been simulated, the magnitude of the subsidy implied suggests that it could be helpful in reducing industry losses. However, as was found with the certificate, the gains are too widely shared to benefit substantially the nonviable thrift institutions. Moreover, Congress did not choose to include the provision in the 1981 tax bill, even though it considered and approved other measures relating to thrift institution taxation, so it is unlikely that rescission of the carry-back rule would occur soon enough to help. And finally, it is possible that the most troubled institutions will recover all taxes previously paid by 1982 even under current law.

Direct Lending

During earlier bouts of depressed earnings, thrift institutions increased their borrowing from both specialized agencies and others. But those were primarily crises of illiquidity triggered by disintermediation under rigid deposit rate ceilings. Access to borrowed funds can improve liquidity, but whether earnings can be substantially increased is less certain when interest is charged at market rates.

Federal Home Loan Bank System Advances

Loans to thrift institutions from Federal Home Loan Banks are not intended as a subsidy. The rate on advances is determined by, among other factors, the system's own cost of borrowing. This rate also reflects the greater security and liquidity of federal agency issues compared with the debt of an individual institution.[44] As a result, the average rate on advances outstanding in July 1981 was 12.93 percent. New advances that month were made at a rate of 17.70 percent, while jumbo certificates of deposit were at 18.90 percent, if they could be sold at all. So these advances are a desirable source of purchased money, although institutions would much

43. Author's estimate.
44. Under the Rate Control Act of 1969, the Treasury may purchase up to $4 billion of Bank Board debt if the ability to aid thrift institutions is substantially impaired by monetary stringency or rapidly rising interest rates. In 1971, the Federal Reserve began trading federal agency issues in open-market operations, increasing their liquidity. And since 1975, Bank Board securities can be issued through book entries into the Federal Reserve's wire system. U.S. League of Savings Associations, *Fact Book '80*, p. 99.

prefer to generate cash flow through lower-cost deposits; for example, even money market certificates at the time cost only 14.65 percent.[45] The twelve regional banks in the system made $6.8 billion in net new loans during the first half of 1981 and another $8.0 billion during the months of July, August, and September.[46] But the benefits are not unlimited. Each district bank sets its own lending terms, which generally restrict the purposes to which advances can be put. In June 1981, for example, the Federal Home Loan Bank Board adopted a policy for the regional banks of granting advances primarily to cover withdrawals. This represents a shift in emphasis away from using the advances to fund new mortgages. And as the Bank Board's older obligations mature, the interest rate will approach market levels. During 1981 and 1982, the value of the lower-rate advances outstanding to savings and loans could approach $1 billion, an amount already incorporated in estimates of industry earnings. Inasmuch as new borrowing must be at market rate, however, there is no possibility of increasing the figure.

Direct Market Borrowing

Most mutual savings banks do not have access to Federal Home Loan Bank advances, and so rely on borrowing in the public market. Savings and loans also engage in a substantial volume of such borrowing, although it accounts for a smaller share of their liabilities. Jumbo certificates of deposit, especially when issued in denominations well above $100,000, and repurchase agreements are similar to loans in terms of cost, maturity, and seniority in the event of liquidation. These sources of outside funds may be jeopardized by market fears about thrift institution problems, with the potential of impaired liquidity, especially for mutual savings banks. Borrowing from the Federal Reserve, described below, might be necessary. But as direct borrowing and jumbo certificates represent the most costly sources of funds, the impact of this switch on earnings would be minimal.

Under their charters, stock savings and loan associations may issue new shares to raise funds for investment. Mutual savings banks can sell subordinated debentures. Until recently, however, the rules governing subordinated debt for mutual savings and loan associations were highly

45. Federal Reserve Board, *Statistical Release G.13* (August 4, 1981). Jumbo certificate rate for thrifts assumes a 1.5 percentage point premium over six-month rate for commercial banks.
46. FHLBB, "Savings and Loan Activity in September," table 3.

restrictive. (Under some circumstances, mutual savings and loan associations may convert to a stock charter, thereby gaining access to equity financing.) The Depository Institutions Deregulation and Monetary Control Act (section 407) liberalized the rules, and associations are now permitted to issue mutual capital certificates. These instruments are similar to stock in that they are subordinate to all other liabilities in the event of liquidation and are entitled to the payment of dividends at either a fixed or variable rate. Given current conditions, however, institutions could not successfully offer stock, subordinated debentures, or mutual capital certificates. Their low or negative net worth positions would make these issues unattractive to investors, particularly for the firms most in need of new capital.

Borrowing from the Federal Reserve

New Federal Reserve Board regulations were issued to implement section 103 of the deregulation act. That section requires the Federal Reserve to "take into consideration the special needs of savings and other depository institutions for access to discount and borrowing facilities consistent with their long-term asset portfolios and the sensitivity of such institutions to trends in the national money markets."[47] The program is primarily intended to address liquidity problems, since only short-term Federal Reserve loans will be at more favorable rates: the interest rate will be 16 percent beginning with the sixth month of the loan.

This extension of Federal Reserve credit to thrifts was made in response to specific requests for loans and apparently is seen by the Federal Reserve as a last resort. It will not become a major source of funds. The announcement of the program noted that "deposit growth in the thrift industry has continued over this year and the industry in general has sustained a high level of liquidity." The rules require that the Federal Home Loan Bank Board or the FDIC state "why funds are not available from other sources" before Federal Reserve loans are made to thrifts.[48] Although the recent actions represent a relaxation of the previous strict standards, thrift access to these funds will continue to be restricted.

47. 94 Stat. 136.
48. Federal Reserve Board, press release, August 20, 1981, pp. 2, 3.

Secondary Market Activities

Thrift institutions resell on the secondary market many of the mortgage loans they originate. The thrift earns the fees for initiating and servicing the loan, while the interest rate risk is passed on to the purchaser. This provides fresh capital to make new loans, with the institution earning returns on its specialized knowledge of the residential real estate market. Government agencies, such as the Federal Home Loan Mortgage Corporation (part of the Federal Home Loan Bank Board), and government-chartered corporations, such as the Federal National Mortgage Association (FNMA), are important participants in the secondary market. FNMA held $57.3 billion in residential mortgages at the end of 1980, 5.2 percent of the total residential mortgages outstanding.[49]

The secondary market has been a source of liquidity and fee income to thrift institutions when deposit inflows were weak, but the secondary agencies have their own problems. FNMA obtains funds for the purchase of mortgages by issuing debt. This practice has given FNMA a liability structure with average maturity of nearly three years—shorter than its assets (which average about ten years), but longer than the deposit base of depository institutions.[50] The market value of its liabilities has therefore fallen with the market value of its assets. Its average return on mortgages (9.24 percent in 1980) was comparable to that of the thrift institutions. The average cost of FNMA's debt was 10.11 percent in 1980, well below market rates.[51] So the firm is incurring some losses and holders of FNMA debt are also losers.

Pension funds and life insurance companies have traditionally included mortgages in their asset portfolios. These firms usually seek to match their long-term obligations (liabilities) with their investments. When the benefits to be paid out in the future are defined in nominal terms—that is, they are not linked to the rate of inflation—it is appropriate to follow a strategy that will produce a stream of earnings whose nominal value is predictable. Increasingly, however, retirement programs are promising benefits in real terms. Inflation-indexing destroys the link between long-term assets and liabilities. In the future, pension funds and insurance companies may invest

49. *Federal Reserve Bulletin*, vol. 96 (April 1981), p. A39.
50. Federal National Mortgage Association, *Annual Report for 1980* (FNMA, 1981), p. 27.
51. Ibid., p. 29.

in shorter-term assets that move with the inflation rate, so that when benefits are payable in the future, the accrued earnings are sufficient to meet the inflation-adjusted obligation. The problem is once again the transition. Individuals are demanding indexed pensions, yet the underlying investments are not indexed.[52] Moreover, as with the thrift institutions, liquidation of long-term assets at this time causes the firm to realize substantial accounting losses. (The real loss was incurred previously, at the time interest rates rose.)

Unlike the thrift institutions, however, life insurance companies have reduced their reliance on long-term fixed-rate securities. At the end of 1980, mortgages represented 27.5 percent of their total assets, compared with 37.9 percent in 1965.[53] While they held 14.8 percent of total residential mortgages in 1965, by 1980 they held only 3.5 percent of the total.[54]

In the current crisis, proposals have been made for injecting funds into cash-short thrifts. The Federal Home Loan Mortgage Corporation has implemented a program to exchange low-yielding mortgage loans held by thrift institutions for mortgage-backed securities of an equivalent market value. The securities can then be used more readily than mortgages as loan collateral, investments, or liquid instruments for sale to other investors. These swap transactions were intended to provide $2 billion in improved liquidity in 1981. A longer-range program for 1982 and beyond is also planned, as are similar programs by FNMA.

The emphasis in these programs is on liquidity, which can improve gross earnings through an increased volume of business. However, mortgage lending is depressed as much by the high cost of funds as by a lack of them. Since there is no subsidy contemplated in the swaps, they will have little effect on the longer-term fortunes of the thrift industry. The housing market, however, could be helped in the short run. For the problem thrift institutions, secondary market activities will at best provide the cash to maintain operations until the regulatory agencies can address their more fundamental problems.

52. See Michael C. Lovell, "Unraveling the Real-Payment Twist," *Brookings Papers on Economic Activity, 1:1981*, pp. 283–97.

53. *Federal Reserve Bulletin*, vol. 96 (April 1981), p. A27, and vol. 52 (October 1966), p. 1494.

54. U.S. League of Savings Associations, *Fact Book '80*, pp. 32–33; *Federal Reserve Bulletin*, vol. 96 (March 1981), p. A39.

Chapter Five

Summary and Conclusions

Thrift institutions grew and prospered under a regulatory framework that required them to specialize in long-term mortgage lending and retail deposit taking. The system functioned smoothly as long as interest rates remained steady. When rates began to rise in the mid-1960s, Congress and the regulatory agencies imposed binding deposit rate ceilings on all types of accounts. The intention was to reduce the cost of liabilities for thrift institutions so that they could remain viable housing lenders; the ceilings also sharpened the impact of monetary policy on macroeconomic activity. But this control structure was to prove more bane than boon.

The thrift industry, despite periodic setbacks, gave the appearance of health during most of the 1970s. Assets of the more than 5,000 savings and loan associations and mutual savings banks tripled over the decade, exceeding $800 billion in 1980. The ratio of net worth to assets fell continuously during that period, however, presaging the difficult times to follow.

Deposit rates, which affect the cost of an institution's liabilities, were gradually becoming more sensitive to market changes as the result of administrative and legislative deregulation. Rates of return on the asset portfolios of thrift institutions remained locked into earlier lower levels by the long-term nature of mortgages and by regulations limiting investment diversification. When interest rates rose to record levels in 1980 and 1981, deposit flows and mortgage lending slowed, the cost of funds rose sharply, profits turned negative, and the thrift industry began sliding toward insolvency.

Evaluated at market value, the industry's net worth by mid-1981 was $86.5 billion below the level recorded on its books. Most of that deterioration occurred in the preceding eighteen months. This means that, given current monetary policy, thrift industry losses (after tax) may reach $11 billion over the 1981–83 period. Nevertheless, this is a long-term problem of profitability and viability, and does not affect the routine operation of individual firms. Customers will continue to receive normal deposit and lending services throughout this difficult adjustment period, as liquidity—

the availability of cash to meet ordinary business needs—is not expected to be a problem for the thrift industry as a whole. Potential cash shortages will be avoided through a reduction in new lending and through additional borrowing.

A model was developed to forecast the earnings and financial condition of the thrift industry. Analyses of the results of this exercise showed that structural changes will be required. A sizable minority of savings and loan associations will never return to profitability, even under optimistic economic assumptions, and a much smaller share of mutual savings banks will be similarly affected. More than 400 firms—mostly small and inefficient, but with ample resources—must find merger partners to avoid potentially irreversible losses of net worth. Still others—at least 200, and possibly more than 600 under the worst-case assumptions—will require financial assistance from the deposit insurance agencies to arrange mergers. A few closings and liquidations of institutions may occur. The severely troubled thrifts comprise mostly average-sized savings and loan associations and large mutual savings banks. The difficulties are particularly acute in the New York and Chicago metropolitan areas, and in Texas and Louisiana, although problem institutions are to be found in every region of the country.

The evolution of the industry over the next few years has therefore been largely predetermined, and only the accounting rules that emphasize historical costs have prevented a widespread realization of this fact. It will become increasingly apparent that many firms cannot survive unassisted.

The issues for policymakers are first, to decide whether a consolidation of the thrift industry is desirable or avoidable, given the costs of preserving the existing structure; second, to decide what level of assistance to the housing industry is appropriate; and third, to select a set of programs to achieve the preferred outcomes. Whatever the ultimate decisions, they must incorporate a subsidy for thrift institutions or their insured depositors. So another consideration is who will pay for the accrued burden of losses, since the institutions cannot.

Assuming consolidation is encouraged to proceed, the deposit insurance agencies would play a crucial role. The net cost of required assistance from the Federal Savings and Loan Insurance Corporation would range from $2.5 billion to $6.4 billion. The Federal Deposit Insurance Corporation would be called upon to supply up to $2.1 billion to a much smaller number of ailing mutual savings banks. These amounts are within the overall resources of the two agencies. In the case of the FSLIC, however, the margin is slim, and the number and gross cost of the transactions could overwhelm the agency's administrative capabilities and impair its liquidity. Without an enhancement of its powers, such considerations could induce the agency to select methods of assistance that would be less resource-intensive but also less efficient.

Preservation of the thrift industry in its current form would necessitate large operating subsidies for the next few years and smaller infusions after that. The existence of many small firms does provide opportunities for local control and specialized attention to local needs. The drawback, however, is operating inefficiency. With increased homogenization of financial markets and institutions, and with depositors becoming more aware of alternative uses for their savings, the specialized local thrift institution is less viable than in the past. The industry is about to undergo a major consolidation. This decision was made, explicitly or not, as Congress and the regulatory agencies acquiesced in the series of financial innovations that broke down barriers between markets.

The role of thrift institutions in the mortgage market will also change. The once-strong impetus for home-building subsidies appears to have receded under the pressure of budget restrictions and the necessity of paying small savers market rates of return on their deposits. Housing finance will not be as abundant or as cheap as it was in the past, but the larger and more diversified thrift institutions that survive will continue as major sources of mortgage credit. Expertise in originating mortgage loans is a major asset of the thrift industry and one it is likely to exploit. The industry may engage more in mortgage banking—immediately selling newly written mortgages on the secondary market, earning profits on origination and servicing fees —rather than the more traditional financial intermediation, but it will remain active. New sources of lending and retail banking will move in to preserve service and competition if the thrifts fail to do so.

The major issue is how to manage the transformation. Left alone, most problem thrift institutions would arrange voluntary mergers; many would ultimately fail, requiring the deposit insurance agencies to pay off account holders. This process would take place over several years. At the discretion of the regulators, action could be taken sooner and less expensively to arrange mergers or liquidations. Other policy instruments can and will be used to prop up the industry, principally the tax-exempt savings certificate and deposit rate ceilings. All of these plans share the common ingredient necessary for success: they include a subsidy to offset the losses incurred by failing institutions on their old low-rate mortgages. But the plans are not equally efficient in solving the transition problems of the thrift industry. Meeting that goal will depend on supplying sufficient aid to the firms that require it and withholding it from those that do not.

This subsidy is not a bailout, or at least not a new one. The decision to subsidize failing thrift institutions was made when Congress created deposit insurance; economic circumstances then put the institutions in an untenable position. There is no alternative: a plan that does not contain a subsidy element will not resolve the thrift problem. The policy question is the form the subsidy will take.

The programs in place today will prove adequate to address the problem only if there is some improvement in economic conditions that retards the pace and reduces the level of thrift industry losses. Persistently high interest rates, smaller than expected sales of all savers certificates, or more rapid deposit rate decontrol could substantially exacerbate the difficulties. A prudent and efficient public policy would forthrightly acknowledge the magnitude of the problem and demonstrate an ability to cope with the worst. This calls not for interstate banking, new regulations, or hidden subsidies, but only for an enhancement of the regulatory tools already available: increased flexibility and financial resources for the FSLIC, development of a sound long-range policy for deposit rate deregulation, and implementation of a system by the regulatory agencies for identifying troubled thrift institutions in advance of a crisis. Thus prepared, the inevitable restructuring of the financial sector can proceed with minimal disruption to markets, adequate protection for depositors, and the least cost. Part of this planning may well require new budget authority, but those who are concerned about government deficits should understand that this would represent only an advance recognition of costs that will be incurred, on- or off-budget, in any event.

From this narrow point of view, more tax or spending programs like the tax-exempt savings certificate, whose cost is large and effect diffuse, are not needed. Tax-exempt certificates, inefficient though they are, will return a small number of savings and loan associations to profitability at a substantial cost in forgone tax receipts. By itself, however, this tax provision will aid no more than 15 percent of the firms. Of course, if new deposits are stimulated, liquidity will improve and more funds may become available for mortgage loans.

The major elements in a rescue plan are regulatory. Decontrol of deposit rate ceilings under the aegis of the Depository Institutions Deregulation Committee has the potential for transferring large sums between depositors and institutions. Under the current plan, depositors who are unable to use market-rate certificates or money market mutual funds will receive below-market returns on their savings. In this way, small depositors will pay a share of the cost of assisting thrift institutions. The DIDC can therefore be expected to perpetuate rate discrimination, at least for the next few years. Although complete decontrol by the end of the transition period is likely, the maintenance of ceilings during the interim would be of substantial (and perhaps irreplaceable) benefit to thrift institutions.

After a number of thrifts have been aided by tax-exempt certificates and rate ceilings, the weakest institutions will be left to the ministrations of the regulatory agencies. As was seen, most of the burden will fall on the Federal Savings and Loan Insurance Corporation. Its counterpart for mutual savings banks, the Federal Deposit Insurance Corporation, will be less affected because the FDIC is larger and supervises fewer thrift institutions. The FSLIC has so far pursued a policy that husbands its resources, expending funds only in the extreme cases. Because the agency was not created to preside over an industrywide reorganization, it lacks the financial and administrative resources to take a more active role. The FSLIC has shown an awareness of its limitations, and within those constraints it has performed well.

The most urgent change needed in current policy is an improvement in the powers and resources of the FSLIC. Ideally, the agency would develop a comprehensive program to subsidize, merge, or sell off those few hundred associations that are virtually certain to require assistance. It should proceed rapidly with such a plan, thereby ending the erosion of firms' assets, minimizing market uncertainty, and preserving public confidence in the agency's ability to protect depositors. If Congress should direct the FSLIC and FDIC to give precedence to mergers solely between thrifts and within the borders of single states, it must recognize the additional costs that would be imposed on the insurance funds. What is needed is increased autonomy for the FSLIC and FDIC. The FSLIC could be reorganized as a mixed-ownership corporation like the FDIC. It must have the flexibility to adjust staffing to the level of activity, rather than as a function of long-run governmentwide budget priorities. Both agencies must have either wide discretion in their actions or more money to carry out the wishes of Congress.

In either case, arrangements should be made to bolster the agencies' resources, although standby borrowing authority may be sufficient. Realistically, the Federal Reserve System can be expected to make available to the thrift industry whatever funds are required in the event of crisis, so it makes sense to allay public concern now by increasing the insurance agencies' lines of credit at the Treasury. Both insurance funds are currently adequate to meet the net cost of assistance under even the pessimistic assumptions, but without additional infusions the funds could be illiquid and seriously depleted by the mid-1980s. In recognition of the government obligation to protect depositors and maintain the integrity of the financial system, a direct appropriation to the insurance funds as an alternative or supplement to borrowing authority should be considered. Balances adequate for normal default risk and countercyclical functions should be maintained.

A more efficient financial system would result if the resources of the insurance funds were increased enough to permit more rapid lifting of deposit rate ceilings. But a lifting of ceilings would substantially increase the cost of funds to already strapped thrift institutions. Direct financial assistance would need to increase by $1.5 billion or more, and that would require more decisions of the type that Congress and the regulatory agencies find difficult to make, namely, where to obtain the additional funds that then would be required to pay off insurance obligations.

The government's plan for resolving the plight of the thrift institutions appears to be to allow a contraction in the number of firms, provide moderate subsidies through the tax system, and otherwise to rely on the regulatory agencies to adapt the tools at hand to make the transition as smooth as possible. Inevitably, those programs will need to be enhanced modestly.

Once the issue of nonviable thrift institutions is resolved, the question of the housing industry recurs. Some modest changes to relax credit market barriers, such as permitting more flexible mortgage instruments, are appropriate. Beyond that, economics has little to propose, the issue being one of social policy. Congress may decide that the equilibrium supply of housing is inadequate in an unregulated market and seek to shift the distribution of resources back into that sector. Examination of that topic exceeds the scope of this book. What is important is that housing policy be distinguished from the related, but narrower, task of rescuing the thrift industry.

The dangers are that the pace of thrift failures will exceed the ability to handle them—unlikely, but a possibility—or that Congress will seek to halt the ongoing consolidation of the industry by enacting new programs intended to preserve nonviable institutions, restrict competition, or provide incentives to save at depository institutions. Inaction could lead to additional financial difficulties, but too much intervention would probably be a worse outcome. The thrift industry has suffered for fifteen years because of regulations that sought to overrule the will of the market. It is now undergoing a long-postponed adjustment to market conditions. Painful as the transition may be, to delay it further ignores reality and only prolongs the distress.

Regression Results

Econometric analysis was used in chapter 2 of this study to identify the causes of savings and loan association financial problems, and in chapter 4 to measure the effect of rate regulation on deposit flows. The results are presented in this appendix. All equations were estimated with ordinary least squares. The t-ratios are given in parentheses.

Determinants of Income and Expenses

The data source for these regressions were the June 1980 and December 1980 semiannual reports of income and financial condition prepared by the Federal Home Loan Bank Board. These reports cover the approximately 4,000 savings and loan associations whose deposits are insured by the Federal Savings and Loan Insurance Corporation. Associations with assets in excess of $250 million, approximately 12 percent of the firms, were excluded from the sample.

$$(1) \quad ER = 1.514 + 0.6673 \; STOCK + 0.2933 \; URBAN$$
$$ (10.68) (19.54)$$
$$- 3.055 \times 10^{-3} ASSET;$$
$$(12.78)$$

$$R^2 = 0.164; \text{standard error} = 0.768$$

$$(2) \quad ER = 1.741 + 0.6395 \; STOCK + 0.3015 \; URBAN$$
$$ (19.02) (11.18)$$
$$- 0.01103 \; ASSET + 39.20 \times 10^{-3} ASSETSQ;$$
$$(14.76) (11.24)$$

$$R^2 = 0.194; \text{standard error} = 0.754$$

$$(3) \quad I = 0.2491 - 0.3093 \; STOCK - 0.2592 \; URBAN$$
$$ (10.84) (11.33)$$
$$+ 7.404 \times 10^{-3} ASSET - 25.90 \times 10^{-6} ASSETSQ;$$
$$(11.68) (8.75)$$

$$R^2 = 0.113; \text{standard error} = 0.640$$

(4) $I = 0.3308 - 65.46\ ERDIF;$
          (61.73)

$$R^2 = 0.528;\ \text{standard error} = 0.466$$

(5) $I = -2.146 - 74.91\ ERDIF + 3.266\ NWR + 2.067\ DEPGR;$
          (74.74)   (15.71)   (24.61)

$$R^2 = 0.626;\ \text{standard error} = 0.415$$

where

$ASSET$ = assets less loans in process, millions of dollars;

$ASSETSQ = ASSET$ squared;

$DEPGR$ = ratio of retail deposits in December 1980 to June 1980;

ER = operating expense ratio, expressed as a percentage of assets;

$ERDIF$ = difference between actual expense ratio (ER) and predicted expense ratio from equation 2 above;

I = net income after tax as a percentage of assets;

NWR = December 1980 ratio of net worth to assets, expressed as a percentage;

$STOCK$ = dummy variable for stock charter;

$URBAN$ = dummy variable for urban (SMSA) location.

Deposit Flows at Thrift Institutions

Data for these regressions were from *Federal Reserve Bulletin* (various issues), table 1.16; Federal Reserve Board, *Statistical Release H.6* (various issues); Federal Home Loan Bank Board, "Savings and Loan Activity in July," August 28, 1981, and previous issues; and *Donoghue's Money Fund Report,* Holliston, Mass. The regressions were estimated with monthly data from June 1978 to July 1981, adjusted for autocorrelation.

(6) $SMCTI = 0.4275 + 0.0595\ DIF + 0.2376\ SMAT;$
                    (3.663)   (4.668)

$$R^2 = 0.659;\ \text{standard error} = 0.049;\ \rho_1 = -0.393;\ \rho_2 = -0.374$$

(7) $SMTI = 0.561 - 0.0154\ (RMF - RMCTI)$
                  (2.86)

          $+\ 0.343\ (RMCTI - RMCCB);$
          (5.01)

$$R^2 = 0.549;\ \text{standard error} = 0.053;\ \rho = -0.227$$

where

DIF = dummy variable indicating presence of rate differential in favor of thrift institutions;

$RMCCB$ = effective annual yield on new money market certificates at commercial banks, percentage;

$RMCTI$ = effective annual yield on new money market certificates at thrift institutions, percentage;

RMF = effective annual yield on money market mutual fund accounts, percentage;

$SMAT$ = thrift institutions' share of maturing money market certificates at depository institutions, ratio;

$SMCTI$ = thrift institutions' share of gross new money market certificates at depository institutions, ratio;

$SMTI$ = thrift institutions' share of gross new market-rate retail investments (money market and small savers certificates at banks and thrifts, and money market mutual funds), ratio.

Index

95